Detailing and Improving
READY TO RU

S

by
IAIN RICE

Irwell Press 1994
ISBN 871608-54-6

First Published in the United Kingdom
by
IRWELL PRESS,
15 Lovers Lane,
Grasscroft,
Oldham, OL4 4DP

Printed by The Amadeus Press, Huddersfield

CONTENTS

DEDICATION AND ACKNOWLEDGEMENTS

Dedication

Dedicated Collectively to Alec, Alec, Frank, Mike, Peter, Roger and Tony - the 'Tuesday Night Chiorboys' of the Launceston Model Railway Club. Bad coffee and worse jokes, but some of the models are OK!

Acknowledgements

Thanks are due, as usual, to many people, especially: Frank Watts, for much practical help; To Jay Moss-Powell and Godfrey Hayes at Replica Railways, Graham Hubbard of Bachman Industries (Europe), to Paul Cherry at Hornby Hobbies and Dave Boyle at Dapol, to Steve Woof at Comet, to Alan Gibson and to Paul Stapleton at Victors - for information, models and parts. I'm also indebted, as always, to Alec Hodson at ACE Models, Launceston, for putting up with all the phone calls, the frequent disruption of his shop, and for finding all the bits and pieces for me - yesterday!

INTRODUCTION

One of the best of the old style RTR locos - an original Hornby Dublo 'Bristol Castle', the pride of my tin plate collection.

As with so many aspects of life, I find that my railway modelling tends to come around in circles. I started out in the game with RTR locos and stock, in my case a black Rovex 'Princess Elizabeth' with mushroom collectors below the cab, and a pair of shortie coaches that rapidly went banana-shaped. Twenty years later I'd scaled the dizzy heights of kit building and, in my 'Tregarrick' layout, had a model railway which was almost 100% scratchbuilt. But these days, I'm more than happy reworking and improving Athearn and Atlas diesels for my American HO layout, or modifying Replica panniers and Bachmann moguls for my OO and P4 essays.

Childhood memories are of better RTR models lusted after, and occasionally acquired. There was an original Farish 'Merchant Navy' and 'Prairie Tank', various Hornby-Dublo offerings, especially the 8F, and one or two foreigners from Rivarossi and Mantua; I actually owned one of the famous Varney 'Dockside' Baltimore and Ohio 0-4-0 saddle tankers, lettered, if I recall aright, for something called the 'Great Quiggly and Toddlepool Railway'. Well, I was only ten at the time!

I'm considerably older than that now, and no longer possess any eye teeth to give up; but I still hanker after some of the exquisite products that are

now on offer from the RTR makers, although these days it would be an Atlas/Kato Alco RS3 or a PFM brass Boston and Maine B15 mogul that would see me slapping the knock-down price tag on granny.

I suppose that through much of the time when I was a carefree (if impecunious) bachelor and had time to assemble kits and scratchbuild the odd locomotive, RTR locos were, by and large, in a sort of limbo. On the one hand, there were the old survivors, far more toy than model, which were of no interest to a 'scale' modeller such as I fancied that I'd become. By contrast, most Hornby Dublo locos - not yet the collectors items they have now become - were not so very far removed from a proper scale job, even if the tinprinted stock got a resounding thumbs down. Given the rewheeling treatment, the A4, Duchess, 2-6-4T, Castle, 8F, rebuilt 'West Country' and sundry diesels made pretty acceptable models.

There were signs of a move toward better things in the 1960s, when Tri-ang Hornby occasionally produced some rather better offerings than their rather basic norm: The B12, Britannia, EM2 Co-Co electric, original A1A-A1A Brush type 2 and the L1 4-4-0 were a decided cut above the average Margate product of the time. This er-

ratic dabbling with the fringes of scale modelling culminated in the 'Lord of the Isles' and the clerestory coaches. But Margate hadn't really mended its ways very much; we still had steam-roller wheels and things like the Ivatt 2-6-0 and 'Albert Hall' to swallow.

All this changed in the 1970s. Even Rice, lost in his ivory tower of P4 scratchbuilds, became aware that something pretty fundamental had happened out there in Railway Modellingland. The first time I saw a Palitoy Mainline J72, I couldn't quite believe it. What were these wheels, as close to scale as most of the 'scale' wheels of the day? And these neat wire handrails with the turned knobs? And this exquisite paint job in LNER green, crisply lined and lettered to a standard that only the very best of the DIY brigade could aspire to? And all for, if I recollect aright, twelve quid. This was a long way from the old Tri-ang 'Jinty' we scale buffs loved to sneer at.

The models that followed the original four new-generation RTR locos (Mainline's J72 and BR class 4 4-6-0, Airfix's 14XX and Brush type 2 diesel) built steadily on this foundation. The fine wheel profile was found not to be such a drawback as some pundits predicted, and the running, while still not brilliant, was by and large an improvement on the existing RTR norm, Dublo ring-field motors excepted. Making these models out in Hong Kong kept quality high and prices low - perhaps too low, in the case of the financially disastrous discount wars of the late 1970s, when many of these models were being sold for silly money. An Airfix 'Castle' for six pounds fifty told a sorry tale of overproduction and desperation dumping that could only have one economic outcome.

As well as good complete models, the RTR makers also provided the scale worker with a source of cheap, accurate moulded loco bodies that could easily be mated with the etched chassis then becoming available. It was thus possible to produce very acceptable fine scale models at a considerably smaller outlay in hard cash than was required for a kit, and in a fraction of the time taken for a scratchbuild. This was a development that brought a lot of people into finer scale modelling, and also one that opened the way to more ambitious fine scale layouts than had been possible in the days of almost total reliance on kits, some of which were of pretty dubious quality.

The first of these new-generation British RTR locos that I acquired was a Mainline 'Jubilee', given me by Cyril Freezer when I was working on the old 'Model Railways' magazine. I had no use for this model at the time, but I was deeply impressed by its quality and the way in which it really captured its prototype, which I've always thought the most handsome of the Stanier designs. It has lived on the shelf in my workshop for fifteen years now, setting a standard by which I came to judge my own kit or scratchbuilt efforts, as well as other RTR models. I still have it, although for the purposes of this book AMETHYST has now received the minor reworking I have long promised her, and will one day acquire a proper Stanier tender in place of the incongruous Fowler design with which she came.

There have been some pretty major hiccups in the development of the modern RTR loco. For a start, both of the original players, Palitoy/Mainline and Airfix, became immersed in the financial soup and are out of the game now. Their tooling is distributed in a convoluted and incomprehensible manner amongst their successors, Dapol, Replica and Bachmann, whose ranges exhibit considerable overlap. Many of these models are now being produced in mainland China, not always to the benefit of manufacturing quality. Lima also entered the fray in their own fashion, starting at the bottom end of the market with some crude HO scale offerings, but soon switching the 4mm scale and going gradually upmarket. Their steam engines have, for me at least, never hit the mark that the others have achieved, although nowadays they make some fine model diesels.

Wrenn, soldiering on with resuscitated Hornby-Dublo models and newer introductions in the same genre, went into slow and graceful decline, and as I write this have recently been bought up by Dapol. Many of these Wrenn models are now highly collectable, thus commanding substantial prices and making them unsuitable candidates for upgrading. Trix, always a second-rank operator in the UK RTR market, simply faded away in the 1970s and early '80s, although as with Wrenn, Dapol have acquired the remnants, so some models may reappear. The other main home side, Hornby, also went through a series of ownership and management changes, and after a few wobbles now hold their corner pretty well, although they still don't seem to be able to make their mind up whether they're making models or toys. The quality of manufacture is excellent, but you still find silly compromises and inaccuracies, and much of their engineering seems muddled. Three different wheel profiles on the same loco seems to me to smack of a certain lack of identity!

The most recent developments have been in the matter of drive and running quality. Bachmann have led the way with their abandonment of the 'pancake' 3-pole ring field motor in favour of a flat-sided 5-pole can motor driving a two-stage flywheel worm-and-spur transmission, a system that has brought new levels of refinement and haulage power to the RTR loco. The rest have yet to catch up, though Dapol and Hornby have some very worthy contenders, with sprung chassis to improve pick-up.

The worst of the traditional toyshop compromises have largely been done away with. Even Hornby have deserted the flangeless centre driver and other such anachronisms, and the vast majority (although not all - there are some notable howlers still in production) of contemporary RTR locos are extremely accurate models. But they are mass-produced, with the inevitable concessions to expediency that this must entail. Not every detail can be economically produced or practically included, and while many makers now offer dif-fering versions of the same loco, the infinite variety of the prototype offers plenty of scope for 'personalisation'. And, of course, we're still cursed with that *awful* tension-lock coupling, an alternative to which is urgently needed...

Since middle age has crept upon me, and with it the chilling realisation that Methuselah is mythical and Rice isn't, I have made more and more use of modern RTR locos, as well as coming to appreciate the charms of the earlier dynasty that emanated from Binns Road. These days, wearing my collectors hat (a deerstalker, naturally) I certainly wouldn't advocate two-railing and 'scaling-up' an original Hornby-Dublo loco, although I possess a couple of such specimens from my miss-spent past. But I have done many and mighty things to many of the more recent offerings, while the odd older model that has been taken out of the collectable ranks by being got-at years ago has also come in for reworking. What I have done to these models ranges from a light titivation to a major rebuild to full scale standards in P4, and the techniques I have used to accomplish these transformations are the ones I set out in these pages.

As one who is interested in *all* aspects of railway modelling - locos, stock, trackwork, signalling, scenics and operation - I value the RTR loco highly as a resource I can draw on to free time and cash for other aspects of layout construction. My P4 Cornish china clay branch started out with a pair of converted Mainline 57XX panniers, one modified to round-top cab format as described in these pages. 'Broadwell Green', the fine scale OO gauge project layout built for *Modelling Railways Illustrated* uses a stud of worked-over RTR locos, some of which also appear within. And I'm sure you'll indulge me if I sneak in the odd steamer or first-generation Yankee diesel from my HO Boston and Maine layout, on which *all* the locos, so far at any rate, are from RTR makers. Suitably got at, of course.....

**Iain Rice,
Chagford, Devon,
December 1993.**

Chapter One

EXAMINING THE PATIENT

Time was when most of us, I suspect, regarded a new-minted RTR loco as sacrosanct. The last thing we would have dreamed of doing was to subject it to the most ruthless of critical examinations in search of cosmetic or functional shortcomings, then set about it with snips, files and razor saws in a quest for 'improvements'. But then, chances were that our pristine RTR loco would have been so far removed from accuracy that the possibilities for transforming it into a satisfactory scale model were, well, somewhat remote. There were exceptions, of course; the Hornby-Dublo Castle and 8F were both pretty good, and many such engines received Romford wheels, added detail and perhaps a little slimming of the valve gear, when they definitely looked the part.

Of course, in the glory days of the 1950s and early 1960s, the overall modelling standard wasn't that brilliant by comparison with the dizzy finescale heights reached nowadays. Leaving aside the sort of thing turned out by the truly gifted scratchbuilders like Alex Jackson, Ross Pochin or Guy Williams, most 'scale' models were, well, pretty basic. Such loco kits as there were tended to be rather rudimentary, and were often only approximate in detail and outline, while the range of motors, gears, driving wheels and detailing components to be had was the merest fraction of the cornucopia now available. The sort of information contained in detailed magazine 'Loco Profiles' was also unheard of, although there was the compensation that in many cases one could, if so inclined, go and study the real thing.

A Couple of Healthy Specimens

For the purpose of preparing this book, I assembled a rambling but representative collection of modern RTR locos, some 30 in number, presently scattered about my workshop in various stages of undress or reworking. They cover all current or recent makers and all the main prototype groupings, (not to mention a couple of overseas interlopers) and include both steam and diesel types. I selected a couple of reasonable specimens with which to illustrate this preamble, a Replica LNER B1 and Bachmann's new Class 46 diesel. There were plenty of other equally valid choices, but these two are among the best. Putting them under the harsh light of close scrutiny was a revealing exercise; considered as scale models, there was precious little to complain about in either. Screwing in the eyeglass, one might come up with the following detail observations:

A couple of good examples of contemporary RTR steam locos: Mehanotecnika's USRA light pacific, a low cost model made in the former Yugoslavia for the American market (bottom), and Replica's high quality B1, made in Hong Kong for the price concious UK market.

The Replica LNER B1 4-6-0

As a choice of prototype for the popular early BR period, the B1 would be hard to beat. It is just the sort of medium-sized mixed traffic tender engine that could be expected to turn up almost anywhere doing almost anything. No only is the B1 a practical and versatile engine which saw service over a wide area of the British Isles, from Clacton to Caithness, but it is also, in my book anyway, a very handsome

The Replica B1 is notable for having one of the best valve gears yet seen on an RTR model.

piece of machinery.

Replica's version is a very handsome piece of modelling. I actually rate it as amongst the very best of RTR steam locomotive models; very few criticisms can be levelled at it on any count. It is accurate in outline and dimensions, and is extremely well detailed and finished. And as for the specification, it reads like a prizewinner from the Model Engineer Exhibition: The chassis is a split frame design, having driving wheels of the correct size, spoke and crank configuration, with axle end and balance weight detail. The wheel profile is to a decent fine scale OO standard, with plated tyres, although for some reason the locomotive bogie and tender wheels have rather deeper flanges than the drivers.

The B1 has a fully detailed cab - once remarkable, but now accepted as the norm on RTR locos.

Chassis fittings include detailed brake hangers, although not on the leading axle, where they would presumably have caused bogie clearance problems. The brake gear is completed with the cross stretchers and pull rods, a detailed clip-in moulding supplied separately in the box. The sandboxes and sandpipes are represented, and the bogie has the correct outline and sideframe detail. The cylinders are a small blot, being a tad too short, if otherwise well detailed and of the correct vertical depth and cross section. The rods and valve gear, for so long a weak area of RTR steam locomotives, are quite simply superb. Few kit or scratchbuilt models can boast better valve gear than this.

Above the footplate, the good news continues. Rivet detail, beadings, overhangs and panel relief are all accurately represented, with a real finesse and delicacy to the fine edges. *All* the handrails are of blackened wire in close-to-scale moulded stanchions, very neatly and squarely applied on both my sample engines. The B1 also has the best set of lamp irons yet seen on an RTR loco, made of blackened metal and glued into place individually. The smokebox door handle is also an applied detail, as are the sandbox fillers, two Wakefield lubricators, the vacuum ejector pipe and the reverser reach rod. Detail is complete down to the anti-carboniser boxes and lubricator pipework. There are, of course, full cab fittings, complete with seats, and flush glazing to the cab windows. The only slight reservation I have about the entire body is a slight heaviness about the chimney rim.

The tender, too, is a fine piece of modelling in its own right. The frames, another traditionally weak area on RTR models, are produced in full relief, with superb axleboxes and springs, nice fine full-depth steps, and crisp rivet detail. The only real let-down on the tender chassis are the tender brake

hangers, incorporated with the frame moulding and hence well out of line with the wheels - a compromise unworthy of the rest of the model. The tender body is, again, quite superb, with wire handrails all round, fine step and beading detail, a full complement of front end detail, and separately applied mouldings for the brake and scoop standards. The rear lamp irons are, however, only represented on the mouldings, and the coal load is no better than most moulded coal loads.

The finish on loco and tender on both the LNER and BR versions is, frankly, as good as many professional paintjobs; neat, clean and very fine about the lettering and lining. Both loco and tender are disfigured, as usual, by the gross tension-lock couplings, but these are only held on with a couple of self tapping screws, so are easily binned. The model also suffers from a common blight of so many British RTR steam locos, a dam' silly great gap between loco and tender, no less than 8.5mm in this case. Totally unnecessary - a gap half this size would get the model around any curve that its fully-flanged six-coupled chassis will negotiate. Only the British would try and build what is, to all intents and purposes, a dead scale model, to run on trainset-type curves. Daft.

Running is the only real let-down on this model. Not that it runs *badly* both of my examples perform quite adequately, especially on a decent controller. But the old Mainline chassis design using that cheap and cheerful 3-pole ring magnet 'pancake' motor and spur gear transmission is not exactly a stunning piece of production engineering, and I've yet to meet a truly sweet example. So, unfortunately, the running is rather noisy and not of the smoothest, especially at low speed. This loco could do with a Bachmann-style flywheel drive.

The Bachmann BR Class 46

A rather less obvious choice of prototype, a Type 4 from the BR first generation diesel programme, only recently vanished from BR metals. Not quite as widespread geographically maybe, as the B1 in its prime, the 46's nevertheless got around a fair bit, and to some surprisingly out of the way places; Cornish china clay branches, for instance! However, they are big (11 inches long in 4mm scale), heavy and rather ungainly locos that really only look at home in a main line setting.

Although this is (at the time of writing) a new introduction, much of it is actually pretty old hat, in that the body moulding is basically a revised version of the old Mainline Class 45 that first appeared over a decade ago. That said, there's very to complain about on this moulding, which is characterised by excellent grille and panel work, the key to quality on any model diesel loco. The grilles are extremely effective, as they also incorporate the framing lying behind them in a most convincing man-

ner. Roof detail, too, another key area on diesels, is excellent: crisp, fine, and with just the right degree of 'depth'.

There are two real complaints with this model. The first is the lack of flush glazing, which a prototype such as this badly needs; a scale three inches of depth to the window surrounds where the prototype has less than half an inch doesn't really come up to the 1990s mark - or do justice to the well-detailed cab interiors (complete with crew at one end). The other complaint is even more serious, in that the model incorporates a major error by making the bufferbeams integral with the main body, whereas on the prototype they're integral with the chassis. This cockup - and I don't see how it can be described as anything less, for there's no earthly reason why the prototype arrangement couldn't have been followed

- dates back to the Mainline model, and it's a pity that Bachmann couldn't put it right in their re-tooling.
Still, it gave me something to do!

The bogies and underframe of this impressive model (these 46s are big brutes) are good, though not quite as fine and crisp as the superstructure, another Mainline legacy. The long 1-Co trucks are ingeniously arranged as what, in steam parlance, would be described as a 2-4-2, which enables them to go round the usual silly curves. Fortunately, apart from making the model the very devil to rail up (sixteen wheels no less, floppin' about in all directions), these arrangements don't compromise the look of the model. Less pleasing is a wheel profile considerably coarser than is now the norm among the better RTR makers - oh for a proper OO wheel standard! And, of course, there

are the usual dratted tension-locks, screwed to very obtrusive mounting blocks that get my saw-fingers itching.

When it comes to the running, however, there can be no complaints at all. Bachmann are currently leading the field by a country mile in the RTR loco running stakes, having adopted the drive systems for both steam and diesel locos used for their American market offerings. And the USA long ago ceased to put up with cheap and cheerful mechanisms in anything other than cheap and cheerful models, which most British RTR locos most certainly ain't. So, the 46 benefits from the state of the art drivetrain from the American Bachmann 'Spectrum'GE - 8 40 C -skew-wound 5-pole can motor, twin balanced flywheels, shaft drive to both bogies, 8 wheels driven, 8 wheels collecting. The result is that it runs superbly: quiet, smooth down to the merest crawl, capable of imperceptible starts, and with enough tractive effort (courtesy of a weight of 700 grams, a pound and a half in old money) to pull the side out of the proverbial house. Someone apparently managed 35 coaches with one...

The State of the RTR ART?

From these almost-eulogistic descriptions, you might think that there's precious little wrong with contemporary RTR locos, and hence no need for this book. Would that t'were so, but I fear that the two pinnacles cited above are not wholly representative of the picture. There are many older models still in production that fall some way short of the standards described, while a lot of modellers - including yours truly - probably either own, or tend to acquire, a goodly few elderly or secondhand locos that, while they may be lacking in certain respects, still have the potential to make good models with a bit of work. It's those models with which this book is mainly concerned.

I must confess that I'm not much of a fan of the Mainline style of transverse motor chassis that still dominates the steam outline loco field. I'm even less of a fan of some of the cheap and cheerful tender drive mechs and motor bogies that have been foisted upon us, although Hornby's version isn't so bad

Bachmann's BR Class 46 is a large main line diesel with a state of the art drive system and a body that, while derived from the original Mainline Class 45, is still an excellent example of crisp, well detailed plastic injection moulding. Pity about the lack of flush glazing and that awful coupling.

and can be good. None of these mechanisms, however, can hold a candle to the Bachmann US-style 'flywheel' mechanism mentioned above.

This retains the old Mainline style of split-frame chassis, but uses a substantial enclosed 5-pole flat-sided can motor mounted longitudinally and driving a two stage worm-and-spur transmission through a very large diameter worm which also acts as a flywheel. The result is a performance several leagues in advance of any previous RTR steam loco drive, and as these new chassis can be bought reasonably for retro-fitting to many older locos, I think they're a great advance. I look forward to the final burial of all pancake-motored chassis designs - pancakes, in my opinion, being best when taken with maple syrup and ice cream, and definitely not when stuffed into hapless model locos!

The Rice Fitness Programme

Judging RTR locos really comes down to relating to your own needs and standards - a sort of motive power fitness assessment, if you like. Fitness for what? you may ask. Well, fitness for the purposes to which you intend to put it, for a start - and that includes the way it measures up to the rest of the models in your collection or on your layout. Assessing whether or not a model comes up to the mark depends on having a clear standard that you apply to your modelling efforts across the board, and that standard is, in many respects, a very individual matter. As I've stressed repeatedly in previous volumes in this series, I have found that *consistency* in modelling is an essential component of both visual realism and satisfactory operation.

So, before deciding what, if anything, needs doing to a particular RTR model, it is first necessary to set out a few benchmarks against which to measure your loco stud. These criteria will come under one of the two basic headings of Appearance and Performance. Setting such standards is not always the easiest of tasks, as there are a lot of factors to consider. Cost, time and skill need to be taken into account to ensure that what you are attempting to achieve makes practical sense. It is also necessary to be realistic about what is actually feasible in the context of modifying RTR models; there are tasks that just aren't practicable, and you either have to accept the odd compromise, or look elsewhere - to a kit, perhaps - for certain items of motive power.

One way of setting a benchmark for an RTR loco stud is simply to select the best model in your collection, and aim to bring everything else up to a like standard. A slightly more rigorous approach might start from the basis of this 'best model', and look at how *that* might then be improved, setting this 'better than best' example as the target at which modelling endeavours

are aimed. This was the approach I adopted on my American HO layout, where I took a mildly redetailed Atlas Alco S2 switcher (made in Austria by Roco) as my standard, and reworked other (and cheaper!) RTR diesels to match it as closely as possible in appearance and performance. This last endeavour was no mean task, as the S2 runs like a railborne Rolex.

A very ordinary bench-mark - this Replica 57XX has received a surprising number of minor modifications, ranging from the refining of the chassis keeper plate to the replacement of the tank filler clamp handles. Pity I didn't get the new safety valve cover on straight.

A Standard of Fitness

What the benchmark standard for OO locos has come down to in my case can be deduced by examining a typical Rice-reworked specimen, a Replica GW 57XX pannier. Like the Replica B1, the pannier tank chassis boasts very nice and authentically balanced wheels, with tyres to a most acceptable profile. They have thus been left strictly alone. The coupling rods are of scale size and form, with a working joint, while full brake and sanding gear is present, together with all the other chassis detail.

The Mainline-derived pannier tank body is also as well detailed as that of the B1, but does include a couple of compromises, most notably the increasing of the firebox width to accommodate the motor. There is also something a bit odd about the shape of the dome as rendered by Mainline, on which more later. However, the chimney, that vital arbiter of locomotive character, seems just about spot-on. Once again, the handrails are mostly blackened wire in quite fine stanchions, turned brass rather than plastic in this instance, while pipework and rivetting are first-class. The lamp irons and rear bunker fire iron brackets are the only real detail omissions.

Benchmark Upgrades

To reach benchmark level, my 57XX has acquired brass strip lamp irons - fore, aft and for the spare lamps on

the running plate. It also has the fire iron brackets on the bunker rear, a better safety valve casing, a dome of a more representative outline, and a full complement of wire handrails. The sandboxes now boast a simplified representation of the operating linkages, while there are decent vacuum hoses, steam heat connections and screw couplings on the bufferbeams. The AWS detector shoe and battery box have also been added, and the numberplates are etched brass rather than printed.

The finish has also received attention. The paintwork has been carefully weathered down to a realistic finish, with the coupling rods in a dull oily shade. The driving wheel tyres no longer have shiny front faces. A driver and fireman (or at least, the visible portions of a couple of hapless ASLEF members) inhabit the cab, and the coal in the bunker is The Real Thing.

Toward the Ultimate

I have another RTR-based pannier which also meets a benchmark standard, albeit a rather different one. This example started life as an original Mainline model, quite an early specimen. It has been far more extensively modified than the OO model just described, for this is an all-singing, all-dancing P4 version. This means, of course, that the original chassis could not be used, as it's not really practicable (though I dare say it's possible) to convert these split-frame chassis to other standards or gauges. So my P4 pannier sits on an etched brass chassis built from one of the original 'Perseverance' kits, with beam compensation, Sharman P4 wheels, a milled brass Sharman gearbox and a Mashima can motor. It runs smoothly, silently and very, very slowly.

In keeping with the finescale chassis, the body has been upgraded to the best standard that I could manage. So,

Another 57XX derived from the same Mainline / Replica body moulding is this P4 version built for my Cornish clay branch. As well as a new chassis - from a Perseverance kit - the body has been extensively reworked and re-detailed in line with kit and scratch-built locos used on the same layout.

all the handrails have been upgraded or replaced, using finer wire and scale sized knobs. The injector detail has been fretted-out, and a scale firebox and boiler built onto the bottom of the pannier tank moulding. The dome shape has been corrected, and the chimney profile fined down a touch. Visible edges of the cab cut-out and bunker top have also been thinned down. The smokebox door handles have been replaced with scale items, as have the buffers, safety valve bonnet, whistles and whistle shield, and tanklid screw-down handles. All the sandbox operating linkages are modelled to scale, there is a full complement of lamp irons and fire iron brackets, and extra pipework and lubricator detail has been added. The cab now boast a full set of fittings although, as yet, no crew. The numberplates are brass, and the paintwork is extensively and carefully weathered.

A Pointless Comparison?

Put these two engines next to each other, and the P4 model obviously shades the OO version. It dam' well should do, as it took about five times as long to produce and cost more than twice as much! But put the 'improved' Bachmann model next to the off the peg item, and the difference between

the standard and modified models is almost as marked - all for less than a fiver and two or three evenings. I daresay that several of the extra improvements that I applied to the P4 model could be applied to a OO version - the finer handrails, for instance, and some of the extra pipework. But the really fundamental improvements, to the firebox and boiler, would not be practicable without replacing the RTR chassis; and if you're going to those lengths, you might just as well go the whole hog and model to a more accurate track gauge! Only where the RTR chassis is *mechanically* lacking would I consider it worth the effort of building a replacement.

In my opinion, trying to bring a OO version up to the standard of the P4 model would be as pointless as it is impracticable, as the model would then be inconsistent within itself. I undertook that much modification to superstructure of the P4 version to bring it in line with the finescale chassis, and, more importantly, to enable it to live alongside other kit and scratchbuilt locos on a P4 layout. In other words, the benchmark was different.

Aiming toward some sort of 'ultimate standard' is, I suppose, half the point of P4 modelling. But, by the havers, it don't 'arf take a long time to build locos to look like this, whether by modi-

fying RTR, starting from a kit, or scratchbuilding. In the context of a typical very small, very detailed, (very boring?) finescale layout, the effort is perhaps justified. But outside such a context, I can't see the point of going 'over the top' to this extent. In the context of a fine scale OO layout, where one is perforce swallowing a pretty large fundamental error of 'scale fidelity', I'm more than happy to settle for the achievable, even the expedient, rather than spending long hours in pursuit of the theoretically possible. After all, a P4 loco is not necessarily a better loco; a good OO loco is preferable to a bad P4 one any day, and if the use of OO standards makes a more interesting layout possible, then that's a big plus in the overall modelling equation.

Fitness Assessment.

So, the first concern on acquiring a new item of RTR motive power - or perhaps even *before* acquiring it - is to run the usual critical eye over it, with a view to deciding in which areas of detail or performance it falls short of the standards you have adopted for your own motive power stud. Having just spent a few convoluted paragraphs skating warily around this whole business, I obviously can't be too specific about what will or won't be acceptable.

Prototype Conformity.

One area where it is relatively easy to pronounce definitely as to fitness is in overall appearance. To judge a model's conformity to its subject, there is no better tool than a good prototype photograph or, preferably, set of photographs, depicting a particular engine. When judging the authenticity of models, I'm never too worried if I find the odd dimensional discrepancy with the ruler, but if the basic proportions are out or the model just 'sits' all wrong, then I start to have doubts. Some unsatisfactory visual elements can be corrected, such as when the chimney is the wrong shape or the splashers are too big. However, if it's a model with really basic error, such as the boiler being too small or the whole loco being stretched or squeezed for length or height, then I'm afraid I tend to turn my back on it. My experience suggests that, no matter what you do to a model incorporating such a fatal flaw, a satisfactory result rarely ensues.

As well as looking at the general conformity of an RTR model compared with the prototype, I generally try and go one stage further, and compare it with a particular engine. This can be looked at from both directions; you either start out with the intention of modelling a particular engine, where the need to modify your RTR model is driven by a pre-determined end result; or you look for a prototype example that is as near as possible to the RTR model as produced. Given that many current RTR locos have been based closely on single preserved prototype

examples, this latter approach is often quite a straightforward process. A bit of this sort of prototype research is well worthwhile, as the model that follows accurately a particular engine will be both more authentic as a model, and also far more individual. I'm happy enough to have a stud of RTR-based engines, but I'd far rather that they were all models unique to me, rather than exact clones of the model that everybody else has on their layout. To me, transforming a mass-produced 'pea out of a pod' RTR loco into an individual 'portrait' of a real engine, capturing the atmosphere and personality of the subject as closely as practicable, is the real aim of the game. In pursuing this end, prototype photos are an indispensable aid.

Common RTR Ailments.

Here, for what they're worth, are a few of the commonest shortcomings of recent RTR that I've found it necessary to address in assembling my own stud of fine scale OO locos. Starting with the most simply rectified faults, the remedying of which I classify as 'superficial' surgery, there are a number of almost universal shortcomings. The first of these is, of course, the tension-lock, that carbuncle of a coupling which I miss no opportunity to lambast in my writings. Why we are stuck with this monstrosity I'm never quite clear, given that there are a number of viable alternatives that are nowhere near such a mote in the orb. The Fleischmann style of coupler widely used on the Continent is far less of an excrescence, while horn hook couplers of either the homegrown Peco variety

or the US NMRA version are also a lot more discreet. The trouble is, of course, that the good old British hook-and-chain non-automatic coupling, while perfectly easy to model cosmetically, requires a steady hand, a keen eye and sober habit when used on small scale models. Anything more user-friendly, however, just looks wrong.

My own answer to this particular dilemma is slightly schizophrenic; I prefer to fit proper screw couplings, but find them a pain to use much of the time. So I have also devised my own, rather more discreet, variant of the tension-lock, the 'Bringewood' design described in the fist volume of this series, *Detailing and Improving RTR Wagons*.

On locos, I restrict the installation of this coupler to the provision of the fine wire loop which takes the place of the 'Volvo Bumper' bar used by the commercial tension-lock designs. These simple and relatively unobtrusive wire loops are quite compatible with the commercial tension-locks, which does at least mean you don't have to deface your locos, even if the rest of your stock suffers from this visual blight. The fitment of such a wire loop also doesn't preclude the installation of proper screw or 3-link couplers for either cosmetic or practical purposes. As half my OO stock has 'Bringewood' couplers and the rest has 3-links, I can thus have the best of both worlds whilst seated upon the fence.

The other almost universal irritation is the one I touched on when reviewing the B1 - the excessive gap left between RTR locomotives and their tenders, traditionally associated with 'the need to get around trainset curves'. Leaving aside the twin facts that a) you can halve most of these gaps and still disappear up your own rear coupling, and b) that Hornby, the most trainset-orientated of the major makers, use a closer coupling of loco and tender than any of the 'scale' pretenders, the unhappy combination of an excessive gap with the lack of any sort of fall plate looks *awful*. No full-size locomotive that I know of requires the fireman to be an Olympic longjumper with nerves of steel, and closing up and bridging this gap is an almost instant 'authenticity upgrade' for a lot of RTR locos.

Chassis Shortcomings.

The need to get around diabolical curves also gives rise to a few other common shortcomings on the chassis of outside-cylindered RTR locos: undersized cylinders, missing or misplaced leading steps and, occasionally, bogie wheels several scale inches too small in diameter are all ailments which can be rectified by minor surgery or simple substitution. Rarely is anything too clever called for, and the resulting remedial operations amount to the equivalent of corn-removal for model locos, to be performed under

The vital perspective - here is a real 57XX of the same build batch, but in original condition; no top feed, double hanger brakes. Vital reference if a conversion to this condition is contemplated.

Hornby's 28XX - a last minute aquisition as this book was being prepared - has cylinders of scale size, but the usual over-scale pony truck wheels, necessitating a bite out of the cylinder fronts. A prime candidate for a front end upgrade. Full marks to Hornby for an excellent GW cast iron chimney.

to cylinders, valve gear or bogies.

Bogie and carrying wheels seem to be a particular case of weakness on many RTR locos - even where the drivers are quite acceptable, these carrying wheels are often a bit lacking. There's a peculiar tendency to make them to a coarser profile than drivers, while on many of the locos made in the Far East the centres of the bogie wheels are moulded integrally with the axles. These can be OK, but an alarming degree of wheel-wobble often manifests itself. Which is a pity, as these wheels, which are generally fitted with quite presentable metal tyres, are otherwise pretty satisfactory. Fortunately, it's usually not too much of a job to put things right or shove in something better.

In one or two cases, the actual bogie or, more specifically, its means of attachment to the rest of the loco, also leave a bit to be desired. It's essential that bogie wheels revolve freely, which means that the bogie needs to carry a bit of weight, either within itself, or by transferring part of the weight of the loco to it. Quite a lot of RTR loco bogies do neither, which can result in skidding wheels and a very 'floppy' front end to the loco. Few British RTR locos can equal my El-Cheapo - £25 brand new! - HO 'USRA Pacific' (made in Yugoslavia by Mehanotechnica) in this respect; it has a very neat bogie springing and guidance system that gives excellent tracking even on 18 inch radius curves.

There is, unfortunately, no properly laid out standard for OO gauge wheels and track, although as I write these lines the newly-formed OO Gauge Association (OOGA?) is addressing the matter. While a goodly proportion of the driving wheels on most modern RTR

steam locos are to a very acceptable profile, which should work well enough in conjunction with finescale OO track, a few do come with rather chunky flanges.

If the loco is of the variety propelled by the Herr Doktor Diesel's internal combustion, then it matters not how dire the wheels are, as Ultrascale make excellent drop-in conversions to fine OO, EM or P4 standards, which enable the situation to be remedied in moments. Regrettably, as yet, the only steam loco for which they have made a like conversion is the excellent Dapol ex-L&Y 'Pug'. One or two other Dapol and many of the old Airfix locos can, however, be quite simply rewheeled using standard push-fit 4mm fine scale wheels. For the rest, a comprehensive range of conversion components is, apparently, on Ultrascale's drawing board as I write this.

Mechanical Disorders.

One of the most intransigent aspects of most modern RTR locos is their mechanical design, particularly where the chassis is of the transverse pancake motor variety. These are not really all that satisfactory, added to which it's difficult if not impossible to make any fundamental improvement. The best you can do is to fine-tune the mechanical bits you've been foisted with to give the best performance of which they are capable. With these designs, such options as, say, re-gearing for slower running speeds or substituting a higher quality motor are just not open.

This is in direct contrast to the old traditional Triang type of RTR chassis, where you could very simply go from a 20:1 to a 40:1 reduction ratio, or re-

place the three-pole X04 with a five-pole alternative. Hornby-Dublo and Wrenn chassis are likewise easy to re-work and improve, while some of the older Airfix models had chassis of a not dissimilar type which can be got at. Unfortunately, many other Airfix locos had a dire form of tender drive, an object which in my opinion is best towed a long way out to sea and sunk by naval gunfire. Or torpedoes - I'm not fussy.

If, as in that case, you find you really can't live with some of the relatively crude mechanisms that have typified many RTR locos of the last decade, then it's almost always a case of binning the RTR chassis and brewing your own. There would seem to be a gap in the market here for higher quality mechanisms for popular RTR locos, and it surprises me that nobody seems to have gone into this 'running upgrade' business. It's very big in the USA, where firms like Proto Power West, Hobbytown, North West Shortline and Heiden make a living providing better drivetrains for Athearn and other RTR models.

We Brits, as so often, are a bit hair-shirted about the whole mechanism replacement business, and prefer to do it the hard way with etched brass chassis kits. Not that there's anything wrong with these - I'm a great user of them, but they are not everybody's cup of tea. However, if you are faced with a really naff RTR chassis, and Bachmann can't come to your rescue with one of their new flywheel drive mechanisms, then there's really no alternative to tackling one of these kit jobs.

Along with all forms of mechanical jiggery-pokery, etched kit replacement chassis fall outside the scope of this book, but a volume devoted entirely to the upgrading, fine tuning, remedying, rewheeling, and even total replacement of RTR chassis is scheduled to make an early appearance in this series of *Modelling Handbooks*.

The current volume, so far as locomotive mechanisms are concerned, limits itself to those modifications and additions intended to improve the appearance of the chassis rather than its performance.

Cosmetic Plastic Surgery.

As with the clinical variety of plastic surgery, the sort of cosmetic rectification applied to RTR loco bodies can range from the eradication of minor blemishes through a 'nose' job - or, in this case, more of a 'chimney' job - to the sort of reconstruction operation needed to put right some fundamental deficiency in the superstructure. I'll leave you to work out the human equivalent of that!

Given that, with virtually all modern RTR locos, we are working with plastic mouldings, then there is almost nothing that isn't possible along the lines of cutting/joining/splicing, and

I have set about a couple of fairly major reworkings of this sort later in the book as examples. The Americans are dab hands at this sort of caper, and think nothing of chopping up and knitting together half a dozen different body mouldings - usually for diesels - to produce some variant as yet unavailable on the RTR market. Be warned, though; the week after you finish just such an exhaustive re-hash, Bachmann will bring out the very model you've just sweated blood over!

The sort of thing that I'm on the lookout for when assessing the need for plastic surgery on RTR locos are - oversized or misplaced splashers, missing bits of boiler, untoward bulges, bad mould part or step lines, shallow and unconvincing detail, over-thick cabsides and the like, and poor or inaccurate boiler fittings. It always amazes me just how inconsistent the various makers are in this last respect; I mean, if they can get one chimney right in a range, why not all of them? But no; Mainline, for instance, who, with the N2, 56XX, pannier and Jubilee, produced some of the best boiler mountings ever to grace an RTR loco, also inflicted on us some of the worst, such as the excrescences that so disfigured their 43XX Mogul and Manor 4-6-0. Airfix were a like case - lovely, fine, accurate outlines on the 4F, the Castle and the Dean Goods, but an 'orrid approximation on their best-selling 14XX.

As always, nothing, but nothing, is sacrosanct in my eyes. I view everything with the cold critical eye of disfavour. The famous Rice rhetorical question hangs ever on the lips: is this as good as it could be, or could I make it better? The answer is that if it doesn't look right, then out come the files, the razor saw and the Stanley knife. Paeans of praise are, as usual, offered up to the makers of Plastikard and Milliput, those two indispensable aids to the successful mutilation of moulded plastic models.

Details.

As well as seeking to eradicate faults in, or improve in some way upon, the basic moulding of the loco superstructure, the other main area for attention is the applied detailing of the model. This is an area where, for reasons of production expediency, the RTR maker usually has to brook some compromises, compromises which are often easily done away with. As well as the upgrading of basic detailing, there are two further aspects to consider: the addition of detail that the RTR maker, for some reason or other, has left off; and the altering of detailing to follow a specific prototype engine.

Much of this work might come under the misunderstood and overworked heading of 'superdetailing'. This is yet another of those meaningless terms that the hobby seems to have acquired back in the 1950s. According to my well-thumbed 'Concise Oxford', the prefix 'super-' means 'exceeding, going beyond, more than, transcending, too exalted for contact or connexion with'. If you're simply adding detail, it's difficult to see how you can be exceeding or going beyond anything, although perhaps the bit about such detail being 'too exalted for contact' explains why so many of the bits I used to stick onto my battered efforts used to promptly fall off again!

I suppose that in those days, when the presence of such fundamental bits of locomotive anatomy as bufferbeam hoses, brake gear or handrails gave rise to gasping awe, then the coining of the description 'superdetailed' to mean a model which went beyond the barest basics made some sense. By the standards of my miss-spent youth, however, virtually any current RTR model is 'superdetailed', to a degree that would have seemed inconceivable not so very many years since. So, to some extent, anything that we do in this direction will be rather along lily-gilding lines.

Nevertheless, there are a few lilies about that can take a bit of gilding, and the detailing of RTR locos is definitely an area where the appraising eye can suggest worthwhile improvements. The replacement of moulded-on handrails, grabs or pipework with proper 3-D items in wire, the application of extra pipe detail, the installation of lifting eyes, ringbolts and brackets and that old favourite, the provision of a full set of lamp irons - these are all jobs worth tackling. The proper modelling of of these prototype fittings are typical of the tasks that RTR makers have to skate over to some extent. Even such simple upgrades as the replacement of a too-uniform moulded coal load in a tender with a carefully placed teaspoonful of the real thing can make a worthwhile difference, particularly if you've several specimens of the same tender on the layout. Nothing looks less convincing than two or three tenders with identical coal, lump-perfect in their correlation!

Finish.

The other aspect of RTR locos which I find I always want to do something about is the finish. Again, this is an area where personal preferences and aims will come into play, so I'll nail my colours to the mast at the outset: I'm after realism, atmosphere, the feel of the soft sulphurous gritty environment that the steam loco created. Sure, I like to see a clean loco, shiny paint and all - but I like it to look like a real loco that's been used and cleaned, not some piece of shiny idealism straight out of the toyshop window. So all my locos, together with the rolling stock, structures, vehicles and all the other elements of my layouts, are carefully weathered and subtly toned to look as natural as possible.

This is not the easiest of procedures to describe, but with the help of the colour section I hope to convey the sort of effects I'm after, and just how I go about achieving them. It's an area of the whole business of reworking RTR models that I find especially rewarding, as nothing takes away the 'toy' look more certainly than a well-executed weathering job, even if all else is left as the RTR maker intended. Combine it with some remodelling and detailing, and the resulting model can quite belie its mass production origins.

In the Final Diagnosis.

At the end of the day, then, what can we expect to find 'wrong' with a typical modern RTR loco? And what remedies will need applying to bring it up to our benchmark standard? Obviously, no fixed answer is possible, but a representative prognosis for a loco requiring the full works might run thus:

Superstructure - eliminate any mould marks, pierce any openings that are closed over, thin down visible edges; correct any errors such as oversized or misplaced splashers; refine or replace boiler fittings; refine, reposition, add or replace moulded steps; replace or add moulded-on or missed off handrails and pipework with wire or wire and turned knobs; upgrade bufferbeam hoses, fit scale couplings if possible, maybe fit turned or sprung buffers; fit metal strip lamp irons, add lamps as appropriate; add any missing detail such as stay brackets, lubricators, AWS gear. etc; glaze cab windows, detail cab, hire crew; close up loco/tender gap, fit fall plate; coal up tender or bunker with real coal and provide fire irons and coal-watering hose.

Chassis: get rid of horrible tension-lock couplings; fit scale size cylinders if required; reduce oversize flanges on wheels if possible; rewheel diesel power bogies; fit decent carrying wheels; improve bogie detailing or replace bogie/pony truck with etched or cast alternative; fine down over-chunky valve gear; improve brake and sanding gear detail; add missing chassis detail, eg guard irons, AWS shoes, water scoops, plumbing, and so on.

Finish: touch-in and make good any paintwork damaged by modifications or additions; paint additions; add variegation to paintwork by differentiating shades; improve chassis painting, eradicate shiny wheel rims and other anachronisms; pick out or otherwise improve detail painting; tone down factory finish and apply realistic weathering. In other words, the chances are there will be plenty to do!

All-in-all, quite a tall order. But, before we go whaling in with the razor saws and scalpels, we had better decide what else is needed by way of tools, equipment and materials.

Chapter Two

EQUIPPING THE SURGERY

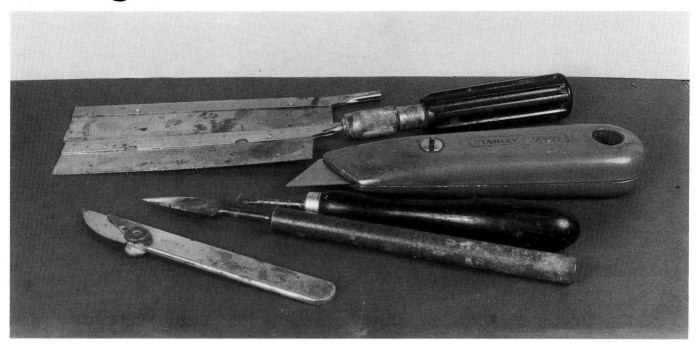

Before moving on from the diagnostic and prescriptive stages to the actual work of remedying RTR loco shortcomings, we'll obviously need to consider what equipment and materials will be needed to accomplish the task. Given that for most of this work we're basically dealing with plastic mouldings, then obviously the requirements in the equipment direction will be pretty much as suggested in the two previous volumes in this series dealing with RTR and Plastic Kit wagons. While I certainly don't want to keep boring regular readers of these diatribes with parrotic recitals of the same old tool list, as each book must also stand alone then I do have to address the topic. So, if there is an element of ho-hum (yawn!) about this Chapter, apologies. Lest you be tempted to skip this section altogether, however, be warned: there are quite a few extra tools needed when dealing with locos that wagoneers can disdain, while I've discovered a few goodies missed from earlier books.

Cutting Tools

One of the jobs that seems to be called for quite often when dealing with RTR steam locos is the delicate removal of mould part lines from boiler and firebox tops, chimneys, domes and safety valves. While quite a lot of this work can be accomplished with a sharp craft knife and small files, there is no doubt in my mind that the best implement is a small, sharp three sided scraper, such as the retractable type sold by Shestos as their catalogue number 1032. This tool enables you to get right into corners and angles, and will take off flash and mould marks with only minimal damage to the paint. The other

non-conventional cutting tool I often call on is a small sharpened screwdriver, very good for cutting into square inside edges such as footplate angles. Mine is actually a leather-tooling chisel, which amounts to much the same thing as a stoned-up screwdriver.

Otherwise, the normal sort of cutting tools familiar to most modellers will serve well enough when working-over RTR loco bodies.
A couple of knives, to start with: a good small craft knife, for which my preference has always been the Swann-Morton brass handle job fitted with the No.2 curved blade, plus a rather heftier knife, the Stanley No.199 with short straight blade. Add on a small selection of saws, the main ones being an X-Acto razor saw, with the deeper type of blade, an ordinary junior hacksaw, and, for some of the trickier carving-about described in Chapter 3, a piercing saw with some coarse(ish) blades. The other useful sawing implement is

Shaping and Finishing

The cutting armoury is rounded out with some small files and abrasives. For files, my usual choice is a flat second cut 6 inch with at least one blind (toothless) edge, plus round, half round, square and triangular needle files. For working with plastics, you don't need high quality needle files, and the cheap Chinese jobs that come in a wallet of six for a couple of pounds will do all that's required. Also useful for getting into odd corners are a couple of 'rifflers' - small files either end of a handle, with a curved shape that will get into most places. The most useful ones are the tapered flat and the triangular.

Abrasives are for shaping and final smoothing, and when working with plastics wet-and-dry papers used wet will give the best results. I use relatively coarse grits, as fine grades of paper will clog rapidly with the soft

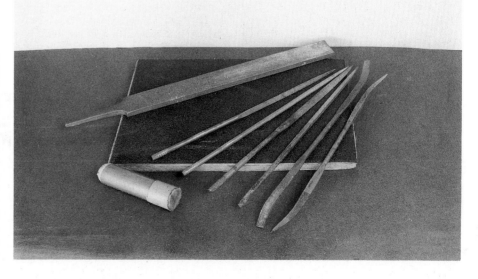

plastic. 180, 320 and 400 grit papers serve me well, and I make my usual taper-ended and flat rubbing sticks by sticking them to small pieces of stripwood with contact adhesive. Also essential is that other stalwart of the plastic modeller's armoury, the sand-

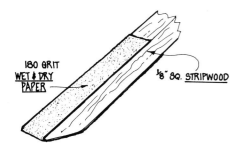

ing board. This is simply a smallish (mine are about 3in. x 4in.) offcut of flat, smooth-faced board such as MDFB, to which is laminated wet-and-dry paper in suitable grades. I use a coarse - 180 grit - board, and a fine one with 400 grit; the paper is stuck with Evo-Stik in both cases. The other useful abrasive for plastic models is a fibreglass burnisher, good for removing unwanted lettering and lining as well as smoothing plastic surfaces and burnishing metal fittings.

Drilling

The other common job when re-working RTR bodies is the need to drill holes, often quite small holes. Power drills, even quite sophisticated mini-drills such as the Dremel, are pretty well useless for this work as they generally run far too fast and are heavy and clumsy in the context of a very small drill bit. There's no need for power anyway, as a pin-tongs or small Archimedean drill propelled by finger power will do all that is required, especially if you lubricate the job with a spot of Fairy Liquid. I've previously expounded my Caledonian approach to small drills, which are fragile and, if in the Imperial number series, very expensive. I get by with a very limited selection of metric drills and a set of fine taper broaches, which enable me to open holes up to any required size. My drill selection is usually 0.5mm, 0.7mm, 0.9mm, 1.2mm and 1.5mm.

The broaches come as a set from Shestos and other tool merchants, generally in a set of 6 in a little plastic wallet. I use the Shesto reference 2193 or 2194 set, which go from 0.4mm - 1.4mm or 0.6mm - 2mm respectively.

Gripping and Snipping

The other main requirement for modelmaking work of all sorts is the ability to grip, snip and form things. A pair of tweezers, some fine pliers and some small snips are the basic essentials. For tweezers, I've always got along well enough with the most basic type of Jeweller's fine pointed stainless steel tweezers, which only cost a couple of pounds. There's really no point in lashing out on anything classier. The fine pliers are a rather different case, as here I have found that good quality pays off. For the sort of work described in this book, a decent pair of fine snipe-nose pliers are essential, while a reasonable pair of round-nose pliers for forming handrails, grabs, lifting eyes and so on are useful. If you lash out serious coin on anything in the toolbox, make it the snipe-nose pliers, which need to be box-jointed and of a good make. CK, Asker, A. H. Dahms and Lindström are the ones to look for, and expect to pay between ten and twenty pounds. If you go for the top range Lindström you'll pay twice that.

For the small snips, there's one tool that beats the rest hands down unless you're working with hardened steel wire. (I don't - not when modifying RTR locos, anyway.) These are the Xuron 'rail nippers', made in the USA and imported into this country by ACME Models - see sources index. These neat, well made shears give a square-ended cut in wire and strip, and enable you to get in very close to surfaces, corners and edges. They are also very good for trimming and nibbling plastic mouldings generally, and are the quickest way I know of doing away with tension-lock coupler mountings, gone in one satisfying Crunch!

The other gripping need that may overtake you when monkeying around with RTR loco bodies is the need to hold the whole thing firmly while you're attacking it. While it is *sometimes* possible to clamp a loco body in an ordinary bench vice, this approach will usually be less than ideal - especially

if the vice is fitted with serrated jaws. I find that an offcut of wood shaped to be a tight fit inside the body moulding is often a far better bet; if needs be, this can then be clamped in the vice. I do occasionally find that I need to grip cast chassis blocks in a vice for sawing or filing, so it's something you will almost certainly need when working on RTR locos. My vice is a Record No.0, which has two-and-a-half inch serrated jaws; I have a couple of short offcuts of soft aluminium angle for use as vice cheeks when gripping things that these jaws would otherwise mark.

Mechanical Tools

Stripping down and re-assembling RTR locos will involve the removal of small screws, so some suitable screwdrivers are need. These days, with many RTR models being held together with small crosshead self-tapping screws, then crosshead (Phillips) type screwdriver bits are as essential as the normal cross-slot type of blade. You can buy a perfectly adequate set of made-in-Taiwan screwdrivers containing both types in a little blue plastic box with a clear lid - virtually every market stall tool trader seems to sell these, along with the Chinese needle files already mentioned. They are pretty cheap, and will serve well so long as you recognise that they are not of a good grade of hardened steel, and can therefore be bent! From the same source comes a similar set of miniature sockets on screwdriver handles. These are for metric nut sizes, and are useful if you're working with US or Continental models.

If you're faced with the need to grip a small nut while dismantling or re-assembling an RTR loco, never use your best fine-nose pliers for the job, as you can overload these and put the tips out of alignment, thereby ruining them for their proper purpose. A small pair of square-ended pliers is a much more suitable implement if you need to grip something like this and you haven't got a suitable miniature socket. Good tool merchants stock proper BA mini-socket spanners with a quarter-inch drive, using a screwdriver type handle. These are the bees knees, and are not unduly expensive. I have them in 6BA, 8BA and 10BA sizes, and metric equivalents are also available.

Soldering Equipment

You can do an awful lot to RTR locos without going near a soldering iron, but there are some jobs for which a spot of heat is needed. The two main operations for which the soldering iron is used are, unsurprisingly, soldering, and less usually, the melting-in of metal detail to plastic mouldings. Soldering operations on RTR locos usually amount to little more than the need to unsolder and re-make electrical connections, although every now and then a spot of minor fabrication, as of hand-

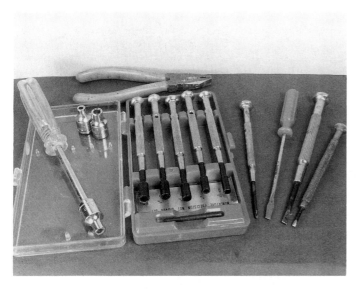

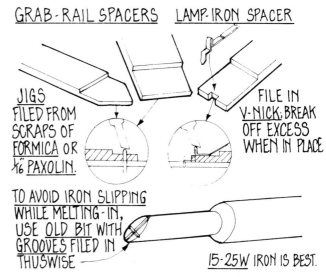

GRAB-RAIL SPACERS   LAMP-IRON SPACER

JIGS FILED FROM SCRAPS OF FORMICA OR 1/16" PAXOLIN.

FILE IN V-NICK; BREAK OFF EXCESS WHEN IN PLACE

TO AVOID IRON SLIPPING WHILE MELTING-IN, USE OLD BIT WITH GROOVES FILED IN THUSWISE

15-25W IRON IS BEST.

rails or pipework, might be called for. A smallish instrument iron such as the Antex 25W is ideal, preferably used with a stand and cleaning sponge. An appropriate choice of solder and flux is dealt with in the 'materials' section.

The melting-in technique is one I use extensively for detailing RTR models of all sorts, and here I find that a smaller and lower-powered instrument iron such as the 15W Antex is more appropriate. I now keep an iron especially for this work, with the bit modified to suit as in the diagram. The melt-in aids and jigs also shown in this sketch are filed up from scraps of Formica, and make the whole process a lot less chancy and a lot more consistent. (If you find you're suddenly suffering from a spot of deja-vu then relax, as this diagram also appeared in the Plastic Wagon Kits book in this series.)

Sundry Implements

Most of the other implements that I have found useful when converting and generally messing about with RTR locos are either basic measuring and marking aids such as six and twelve inch steel rules, a small engineer's square, a small piece of plate glass and a scriber, or various non-specific odds and ends pressed into service as the need arises. Small blocks of wood, rub-

ber bands, sticky tape, Blu-Tak, bull-dog clips and clothespegs can all be valuable aids from time to time. For applying glues, fillers and lubricants, poking out holes, scratching your ear and half a hundred other tasks, the common or garden party cocktail stick is also indispensable. A packet of them should remain in the toolbox at all times. The only other modelling aid that proves vital is a copious scrapbox into which all the odd bits and pieces that 'will come in useful one day' have been thrown.

Materials

Most of what is needed by way of additional material when modifying RTR locos can almost be classified as scrap, as nine times out of ten all that is called for are a few smallish bits of Plastikard. I have a margarine tub into which all such niggly bits find their way, as I find nothing more aggravating than having to cut some soppy little patch of Plastikard a few millimetres by a few millimetres out of the corner of a virgin sheet. Plastikard is, of course, the main material needed for building on to plastic mouldings. A wide selection of sheet thicknesses, Microstrip and Microrod should provide the solution to most structural and detail additions. Plastikard can

also provide the answer for glazing, in the shape of Plastiglaze sheet. This is, however, only 10thou. thick, and I often find I want something a good deal thicker, especially when flush-glazing moulded bodies. The answer is to buy the wife or other loved one some Ferrero Rocher chocolates, and hang on to the clear plastic box in which they come - it's ideal glazing material.

The other main materials required for detailing work are flat brass strip and wire in a wide variety of diameters, ranging from the single filament taken from fine flex to 1mm. diameter nickel silver or brass rod or fine capillary tube. I find that I need both hard-drawn brass or nickel straight wire and a nice, soft malleable copper in as many diameters as possible. The only thing I steer clear of is hardened steel wire, sold as piano wire. This doesn't bend, will wreck all but the best hardened-jaw cutters, and is apt to spear you painfully in the finger at every opportunity. The flat strip is usually needed for lamp irons, and I go for what is often described as 'boiler band strip', around 10thou. thick and about 0.8mm wide.

The odd piece of sheet metal may also be needed from time to time, but once again I almost invariably find what I need in the scrap box. If you don't *have* a scrap box, then a good

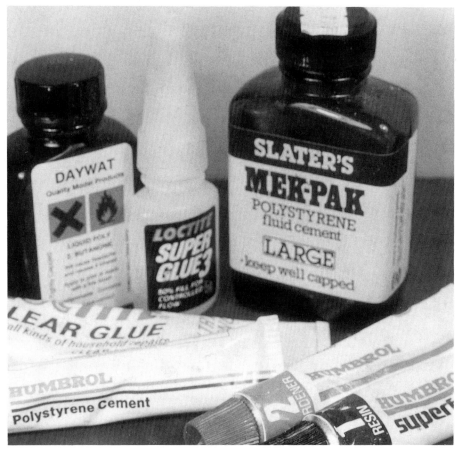

basis to start one off with (metalwise) is a selection of fret waste strips in 10 and 12thou. brass and 18 or 20thou. nickel-silver. A lot of etched kit manufacturers sell bundles of these fret edges at shows for around 50p a go, so acquiring a reasonable stock isn't going to break the bank.

What you may also occasionally need in the sheet metal line, but are only likely to find in the best-appointed scrap boxes, is some etched chequer-plating. Sources of this are in the index.

Fillers

When removing detail and otherwise hacking RTR bodies about, it is occasionally necessary to fill in unwanted holes, or the gaps where your add-on parts don't *quite* meet the mouldings. For this work, I almost invariably use Milliput epoxy putty. This wonderful stuff works beautifully, sticks well to plastic, and can be smoothed with a wet fingertip. Once dry - about three hours to be on the safe side - it can be carved, filed and sanded, and is an excellent modelling medium in its own right. I've made superheater header covers and the like from it before now. For simply filling small cracks or surface imperfections in mouldings, or where a quick-drying filler is needed, I use either Humbrol boddy putty (or Brummer stopping, which appears to be the same thing), or an automotive finishers' cellulose knife stopping, as appropriate. Steer clear of resin based fillers like Isopon or Plastic Padding, as these can attack plastics.

Adhesives

Sticking is the general constructional technique used for most RTR body modification, and a range of adhesives are therefore useful. My basic selection runs to four types: plastic cement, contact adhesive, two-part epoxy resins and cyano-acrylate 'super glues'. For some operations, I find that you need to combine two of these adhesives to get the best bond, as when fixing cast detail parts to plastic. More on that in chapter five.

Liquid plastic cements are the usual choice nowadays, and these are what I generally use for working on RTR loco bodies. There are two main contenders, Slater's Mek-Pak and Daywat's Liquid Poly. Of these two, both nasty organic solvents that need treating with respect, the Mek is the milder, and the Daywat rather more potent and wide-acting. Mek works well on polystyrene, which is the basic material from which moulded plastic models are made. Daywat works on almost any plastic, and will bond ABS and other materials both to themselves and to styrene mouldings. Both will utterly ruin the paint finish and surface detail of RTR loco bodies if used carelessly. The commonsense precautions apply: keep the bottle stoppered when not in use, apply sparingly (I use a No. 1 'Dalon' paintbrush), work in well-ventilated conditions and don't smoke when using solvents. They are both highly flammable and toxic. I anchor open solvent bottles to the bench with a large blob of Blu-Tak, which has to a certain extent saved some heartache

on more than one occasion.

My usual choice of contact adhesive is UHU, although it's getting devilish expensive these days. A small screw-eye to stopper the tube with (as used to be supplied with Seccotine back in the bad old days) is a good idea, as the stuff expands horribly even under mild heating, as when a light bulb shines on the tube. Given that it costs about as much as good malt whisky, it's aggravating to find that a huge blob of it has escaped onto the bench when your back is turned. Yes, I know it comes with a screw cap, but that's far too fiddly to get on and off in the heat of the modelling moment. I apply it with the tip of a cocktail stick, when it does string a bit. I find that a quick twiddle is usually enough to break the thread and sort that out. UHU combines well with liquid polystyrene cements, and I use it for fixing many metal fittings, especially whitemetal castings and etched number plates.

Two-part epoxy resins are pretty useful both as adhesives and also as fillers, and if the parts don't fit too well - as in a shank of something going into an oversize hole - then I always reach for the two-pack. For model work, the quick-cure stuff produces a bond that is more than strong enough, but all such adhesives are not the same. Some, like Araldite Rapid, are 'filled' - that is, they have an inert powder mixed with the resin to produce a stiffish paste - while UHU Strongbond, Humbrol Superfast and several others are neat resin, and thus much more fluid. If you need to fill holes or stick loose-fitting components, then the Araldite is the best bet; but if you want to flow the adhesive into a small gap or crack, or just introduce a trace into a tight-fitting hole, then the runny stuff is preferable. I keep a supply of each type somewhere amid the chaos on my workbench.

The last entrant in the glue stakes is the 1970s wonderglue, the cyano-acrylate adhesive. Once again, we have two formulations, the normal liquid cyano and the thicker gel forms. With this type of adhesive, which cures almost instantly as the bonding excludes air, the container is the crucial thing, as we need to be able to store it without deterioration and apply it very accurately. Steer clear of the little tubes, and head for Loctite 'Super Glue 3' in 5g. controlled flow bottles. This is available in both fluid and gel versions, and if you obey the instructions on the label, these adhesives keep well and don't clog. I always apply cyano indirectly - that is, I place a spot on a scrap polybag (my workbench is always littered with scrap polybags, as every model railway manufacturer known to man packs everything he possibly can in as many different polybags as possible) and use a piece of wire or the tip of a cocktail stick to transfer the required (tiny) amount of adhesive to the job.

Solders and Fluxes

Unless the assembly of a whitemetal detailing or conversion kit is involved, then I usually find that I can get by very nicely for all RTR body detailing work with my usual combination of 145 degree uncored wire solder used with phosphoric acid flux at 'brass' strength, 12 - 15% (see sources index). If I do decide to solder-assemble whitemetal castings, as in the pannier tank conversion described in Chapter 4, then the special lowmelt 70 degree whitemetal solder is required, used with a weaker 6% solution of phosphoric flux. The same sources apply.

When working on RTR chassis, however, the use of a liquid flux (especially a highly corrosive one like Carr's Green Label, which I avoid) for soldering work close to the motor is not a good idea. Liquid acid fluxes should also be avoided when making electrical connections. In these situations, a resin paste flux such as 'Fluxite' is a better bet, used with a cored 145 degree solder. Clean the iron frequently with a damp sponge when using resin fluxes, and scrape off any flux residue from completed joints.

Metal Blackening Solutions

RTR makers are divided upon the matter of finishes for handrails and other turned or fabricated metal details. Hornby generally go down the 'bright and shiny' route, while Replica and Bachmann go for a dull, blackened finish. Dapol go from one extreme to the other, but seem to hanker after chrome plate given half a chance (vide the J94 0-6-0ST 'Austerity'). I have a strong preference for the Mainline style of chemically blackened finish for such fittings, and to achieve this I use 'gun blue'.

This is usually a thin paste sold in tubes or little pots. It can be thinned

The only other things needed to set about RTR loco conversions are, of course, somewhere to work - in this case, Rices tarted up garden shed, and perhaps a few visual aids, fetchingly modelled here by Frank Watts, who has obviously seen something he dosen't approve of.

with water and applied by brush, or the component can be dipped in it. It has a rapid blackening action on steel and brass, and gives a pleasant, 'soft' brownish-black sheen which also provides a good foundation for paint. The brand I use is Phillips Gun Blue, sold in 20g. pots for a couple of pounds. I get it from the local farmers merchants-cum-ironmongers. This is nasty stuff, highly toxic and corrosive. It needs handling and storing carefully, as do many of our solvents and other chemical aids.

Odds and Sods

Leaving aside specialist detail fittings, dealt with in Chapter 5, and

paints, which figure in Chapter 7, then most of the other materials needed for working-over RTR locos come into this category. Plasticene to make a basis for coal loads, odd bits of ultra-fine flex for coal-watering hoses, paper and tissue paper for weather curtains and tarpaulins, thread and fine chain for ropage, small scraps of 1mm. ply for timber cab floors, and a supply of good steam coal crushed and sieved to a suitable size for the scale in use are the main requirements.

I now have a procedure for producing 'scale coal', which goes something like this: select suitable lump - a small piece of boiler fuel or anthracite is best - and place in thick polybag or, better still, wrap in stout cloth. Place coal on granite boulder in back garden, and berate with lump hammer used as a crusher. Keep going until the coal is as small as possible, by which time the polybag will be in some state. Transfer coal to empty margarine tub and fit lid, in which holes of a suitable diameter to pass your maximum lump size have been made with a leather punch. Sieve coal into second margarine tube.
Return residue to crusher, and tip crushed coal into an ordinary kitchen sieve or, in my case, an old tea strainer. Sieve again to remove dust and undersize lumps. Bingo! Scale coal.

Nurse, the Screens....

Having thus equipped ourself for every contingency that might arise during the improvement of our hapless RTR loco, it is now time to set to and start stripping the patient ready for a touch of What the Doctor Ordered.

Chapter Three

MINOR PLASTIC SURGERY

The Mainline - now Dapol - 56XX is an excellent model, and a prime candidate for a bit of plastic surgery. My model started out as a rather tired secondhand example, and received a surprising number of minor modifications to result in a portrait of 5697 in mid - 1950s condition.

Taken at a straightforward cosmetic level, RTR locos fall into two basic categories: those that are accurate in their basic anatomy, and those that aren't. This chapter is concerned with the sort of upgrading work that is involved where the main structure of the model is acceptably authentic, and any surgery is confined to fiddling about with the twiddly bits, such as removing moulded-on detail for replacement or refinement.

For some of the best of the recent crop of RTR locos, the work involved in making really presentable and truly individual models of them isn't that far-reaching. But, that said, there can still be a surprising amount to do. The Mainline/Dapol 56XX illustrated, for instance, throws up a *relatively* short prescription to get it on the line for my finescale OO standard, but even here there are quite a few areas to tackle, with the need to follow a particular example adding several jobs to the list.

A Typical Case

To start with the 'standard' items, which need looking at on virtually all RTR locos, then typically we might need to set about the following list of modifications and additions: the provision of a full set of brass strip lamp irons, the substitution of wire and turned stanchions for any moulded-on handrails, the substitution of better bufferbeam fittings, a change of couplings and the provision of additional cab interior detail and a crew. Other refinements might include the fitment of etched brass numberplates in place of printed ones, a load of real coal, the provision of an appropriate set of lamps, and the addition of a set of very necessary fire irons on tank top or tender.

Staying with the 56XX as an example, most of the other alterations I decided upon were needed to make the model conform to a chosen prototype, No.5697 as running about 1955. This particular engine was unusual in having a low safety valve casing, and lacked the tank top lubricators carried by most of the class. It also had two extra grab irons on the boiler in line with the fronts of the tanks. Being a passenger-fitted example, 5697 has steam heat connections, and is also fitted with AWS gear, the shoe being very prominent beneath the front of the loco beneath the bufferbeam. One of the few omissions of note from the Mainline body are the grab irons on the footplate above the leading steps, so these needed adding from wire and turned knobs. Although this model already has wire rather than moulded grabs on the bunker sides and rear they are rather chunky, so I decided it was worth replacing them with a finer wire.

The rest of the work on the body of my particular 56XX was concerned with repairing some minor damage that the model had suffered before I acquired it; two buffers and the safety valve bonnet were missing (the latter being no loss in this instance), and the whistles and whistle manifold were broken. These latter were replaced by proprietary turnings, while the missing buffers were replaced with Alan Gibson turned spring items. Otherwise, the body needed very little 'tidying'; there was a bit of extraneous moulding flash along the boiler top and a rather visible part line up the front and rear of the chimney, all simple enough to remove.

The chassis did call for a little more

Good though the 56XX body moulding is, there are still some very visible mould part lines to eliminate on boiler top and footplate.

work, however. The first job was, as always, to unscrew and junk the tension-lock couplings, and to replace them with simple wire loops. I also decided that the deep keeper plate beneath the fore end of the chassis was rather an eyesore, so I modified this with some Plastikard to make it less obtrusive. Extra chassis detail included the AWS gear already noted, which called for a bit of carving away of the plastic front frame extension. I'd have done this anyway, to get rid of the rather obvious mounting pads for

the tension-lock couplings, a job that also needs tackling at the rear of the engine. I also elected to replace the moulded-on front sandpipes with wire, and to reduce the depth of the flanges on the trailing wheels a bit.

The Prescription

As always, I have to try and overcome my own twin handicaps of absentmindedness and untidiness with a few little logistical aids - in this case, a suitable box in which to store the part-built model and its components, together with an accompanying piece of paper. This is, in effect, the model's prescription, on which I write a detailed list of everything I intend to do to it together with the sources of any bits needed and the location of the necessary prototype data. This last is essential, for there's nothing worse than being able to see, in your mind's eye, the very picture you need to refer to - which you *did* refer to, when at the contemplative stage of the job - but not being able to recall in which book or magazine it appeared.

My system starts with the box - usually an Athearn freightcar kit box, a splendid and useful receptacle that is one of the bonuses of having a foot in the US modelling camp. Into this I place the prescription, the model, and, usually over a period, *all* the bits I need to complete the job. These days, I never start any project until I'm happy that absolutely everything is to hand, otherwise I find that things can get *very* frustrating. Next door's cat has to sharpen her evasive skills if I come to a grinding halt on the one free Sunday afternoon of the month for lack of some piffling component or other...

Stripping Down

Unless the contemplated rectification is only of the most superficial kind, it will almost certainly be necessary to dismantle the victim of the improvements more or less completely. This shouldn't cause too much difficulty, as most RTR locos are designed to be put together at a rate of knots by Chinese girls in some far eastern factory. Quite a few locos now also come with exploded assembly diagrams, a useful clue as to how it's intended to come apart. Bodies are often retained either by self-tapping screws - steam engines - or by springing the moulding off of chassis lugs - diesels. These two basic methods can be used in combination, with a screw at one end of the chassis, and lugs at the other, as in the Mainline/Dapol LNER N2 illustrated.

Getting some RTR locos apart can be a bit of a Chinese puzzle, however, with inscrutable Oriental cunning employed to make the main body fixing screw look just like all the others holding on couplings, keeper plates and other miscellaneous bits. I find that the best way of trying to decide which screw does what is to take them out

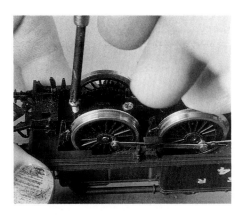

Dapol's ex-Mainline LNER N2 comes apart fairly simply; a single fixing screw at the fore end, and a pair of lugs at the rear of the chassis inside the bunker. Many of the other Mainline-derived RTR models use long screws through the couplings to mount the body - a real curse if you dispense with the couplings, as the screws are then miles too long.

one at a time and look at the length. If the screw holding on a coupling, for instance, is only around 5mm long, chances are that's all it does; if, however, it proves to be 10mm long, it probably has a hidden secondary function. Sometimes the most surprising bits fall off when you remove some screw or other, which is apparently quite unconnected with the part that hits the carpet!

On some occasions, it seems, you can take every dratted screw out of a model and it still won't come apart. Looking for the joining points of the various mouldings can often provide a clue as to how it goes together, and if you insert a knife blade or thin screwdriver and try to lever the mouldings apart (gently!), you may be able to discover the points at which they're fixed together. In the absence of any visible fixings, it's always worth taking off bogies, pony trucks, keeper plates and diesel fuel tanks, as these can sometimes conceal the main body fixing screw. If there proves to be no such screw, try also gently springing the sides of the body moulding apart, or levering the ends out a tad with the fine-bladed screwdriver - some spring lugs are very well concealed. Look out also for models like Lima's BR class 20 diesel, where the buffers must be removed before the body is freed from the chassis. If all else fails, consult your local model shop or phone the manufacturer; someone, somewhere, has got to know how the dratted thing comes apart!

Assuming you can discover the secret of the disassembly procedure, then it's obviously essential to make sure that no components get lost. It's also essential that you know where each part has to go when reassembling the model at a later stage. This calls for more logistical aid, in the shape of small containers in which the various bits can be segregated and stored, possibly with a scrap of paper on which succinct notes may be written as an *aide memoire* for rebuilding. I use empty film canisters to store the bits, and, if needed, a code of little coloured dots of paint to link components, screws and fittings together. You may *think* that you'll remember how it all goes, but if the job is protracted (as it always seems to be chez Rice) then it's surprising how much you forget.

How far the stripdown goes will depend, obviously, on the modifications you intend making. If you're a bit doubtful about things like wire handrails (shall I fit smaller knobs, or shan't I?), then leave them be until you're really certain of your intentions. Rarely can they be re-fitted once removed. On a lot of recent RTR models, the blacked brass turned knobs of earlier models have been replaced with moulded plastic items, which break very easily. If there are moulded plastic detail fittings that have been stuck in place, think carefully before removing these, as they are often located by lugs or spigots which will break off if you try and detach the fitting, leaving only a very poor gluing land for re-attachment. By contrast, turned parts like safety valves, whistles or buffers can usually be removed and re-fitted without difficulty, as they are essentially push-fitted. Use the tweezers or fine pliers to grip the fitting, and twist gently as you ease it out.

Basic Remedial Action

Assuming that you have reduced the loco body to its component parts as far as practicable, then it is time to attend to any minor moulding defects such as visible mould part lines, flash, and rag around the tops of chimneys or safety valve bonnets. For boiler top flash or part lines on steam locos, I wheel on the three sided scraper, which is used across the line of the

fault at an angle of around 45 degrees, working very gently around the curve of the boiler to shave down the unwanted plastic. Often, this is all that is required, and once the surface is flush it can be left. This approach causes minimal damage to the paintwork - once you cut loose with the files or start rubbing down with abrasives, you're letting yourself in for a lot more work at the refinishing stage.

Steam engine footplates are another

area where there can often be mould part lines to eradicate. These often occur either side of the smokebox saddle, where the front part of the multipiece moulding tool locates. Again, the three sided scraper is the tool to use to cut back to a continuous level surface, perhaps finishing off with the taper end rubbing stick at about 320 grit, used wet with soapy water. This gives a nice smooth finish on plastic if you don't rub too hard.

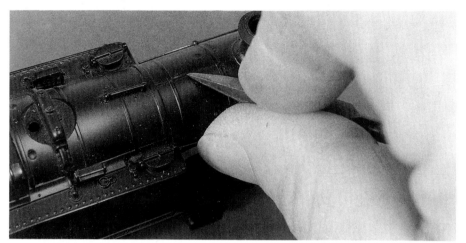

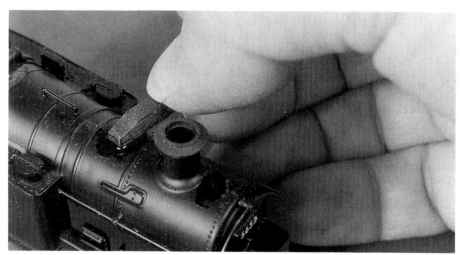

Eradicating a boiler-top part lines calls for careful use of a sharp three-sided scraper, followed by rubbing down with a 400 grit rubbing stick used wet.

Some recent RTR locos made in mainland China have suffered from some rather heavy handed clean up work at the factory. This Bachmann 93XX had a badly scarred firebox and a ragged safty valve, calling for considerable remedial work with fillers, files and sanding stick.

If you've got a lot of material to remove, however, you may need to resort to the riffler files - the flat curved or tapered triangular ones are most useful.

Still on steamers specifically, the trickiest mould line to eradicate is the one that runs up and over boiler fittings such as domes, safety valve casings or chimneys. It's rare for these to be badly pronounced, but I still find it worthwhile removing them. The tip of the scraper will often get in and take off the worst of the line, but on concave curved surfaces such as the seating and rims of chimneys it is often necessary to resort to the round or half round needle file. This can result in tool marks in the plastic, which can be eradicated by wrapping some fine (400 grit) wet and dry paper round a cocktail stick, winding on several turns to obtain a rubbing surface of suitable diameter. Used soapy-wet and gently, such an improvised rubbing stick can smooth away any small surface imperfections.

Diesel locomotive bodies rarely suffer from the annoying presence of flash or part lines to anything like the extent that steam engines seem to. This is probably due to the convenient presence of lots of nice panel joints on the prototype, along which mould joins can be easily disguised. In fact, on only one of my sample selection of diesels, which includes three by Lima, and one each by Mainline, Airfix, Replica, Hornby and Bachmann - can I find any trace of either flash or part line significant enough to warrant removing, that being the mould line down the front corners of the Hornby class 27

illustrated. This was removed with the scraper and a fine 320-grit rubbing stick.

Refining

This is the term I use to refer to the process of 'fining down' some aspects of a plastic moulded body, such as the visible edges to the tendersides, cab, diesel carbody or whatever. These are usually modelled at around a scale 3 - 4 inches thick, rather than the quarter to half an inch of the prototype. Boiler bands, which are often as thin as a sixteenth of an inch in reality, often stand proud of the boiler by several scale inches, while over-thick chimney lips, coarse-edged overhangs and chunky, clumsy beadings, are far from unknown. It's not always possible to eradicate all these imperfections, but there are some dodges that can be used to make them a deal less obvious.

Thinning Visible Edges

To reduce the impact of over-thick visible edges, I often use the old whitemetal kit trick of mitreing the thick edges so that the visible part 'read' by the eye is nice and thin, even if the rest of the moulding isn't. The three sided scraper is, once again, a good tool for this job, and the *modus operandi* is illustrated in the pictures

Thick-edged window openings can be simply disguised by flush-glazing with thickish clear plastic, as described in the section on 'glazing' in the next chapter. Unglazed cabside cut-outs respond well to the mitreing process,

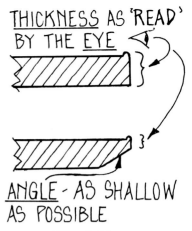

Mitred Edges

The three sided scraper was once again called into play to thin down the very heavy visible edges of the 56XX bunker. On this model, the coal load - complete with bunker extension plate - is a separate moulding - which makes this job a lot easier. On many locos, it would have been necessary to saw out the moulded coal load before any refining was possible.

Getting rid of the prominent mould seam on Hornby's Class 27 calls, once again, for the combination of the three sided scraper and rubbing stick.

21

To retrieve the 56XX bunker extension called for some nifty work with the piercing saw to separate it from the moulded coal load. The salvaged bunker extension could then be cemented in place on the bunker rear.

while boiler bands can be reduced by scraping, filing and sanding. I often do this, as here, while I'm dealing with boiler top part lines. Beadings are more of a problem, as while it's simple enough to reduce the amount by which they stand proud of a surface, it's difficult to make them narrower in section. If I'm faced with a really gross beading, I often opt to remove it altogether, for replacement with suitably-sized Plastikard Microstrip or Microrod.

A slightly unusual modification required on the 56XX was to crank in the front steps, something Mainline apparently overlooked. This was accomplished by filing V-grooves in the rear of the step moulding at the appropriate locations, then bending the steps to suit. The job was completed by filling the grooves with Araldite.

Refining Boiler Mountings

The other area of refining frequently required on RTR loco bodies concerns the boiler fittings, particularly chimneys. There are an awful lot of chimneys on RTR engines that, while fundamentally OK, are just a bit thick and chunky-looking about the rim. If at all possible, I always try to redeem an existing chimney rather than hack it off for replacement, for two main reasons. Firstly, it's generally an awful lot

of work to totally remove a moulded-on chimney, and difficult to achieve without doing a lot of damage to smokebox rivet detail. And secondly, getting as good a fit between the skirt of a cast or turned replacement chimney and the smokebox top as the RTR makers generally achieve with their moulded-on chimneys is no sinecure.

There are, of course, some completely duff chimneys for which there is no hope, in which case major surgery is called for, as described in the next chapter. But in most cases, some careful work with files and rubbing sticks can bring about a total transformation of moulded chimneys, which are rarely *totally* wrong. The Mk.2 Hornby 'Jinty', for instance, looks quite wrong as it comes. Careful comparison with prototype pictures shows, though, that all that is really amiss is the height of the chimney barrel above the rim. These Fowler chimneys have a very shallow lip here - scarcely an inch at full size. Hornby's lip is more like three inches, but filing it down brings about an instant transformation, which, combined with a little work on the rather thick edge of the chimney skirt, gives you a

result that's pretty well spot on.

Over-thick chimney rims are another common failing, and here careful work with the needle files and rubbing sticks, flat and round, can slim down the rim to a more becoming proportion. A good case in point is Replica's excellent B1, which exhibits a rim profile that is far too 'blunt'. The tip of the rat tail (tapered round section) needle file can be used to put in a much smaller radius where the rim flares down into the chimney barrel, which both sharpens the profile and increases the apparent diameter of the rim, which starts off looking too small. A little bit of dressing of the top surface of the rim with a flat file completes the sharpening process, and transforms the look of this chimney. Another common rim failing on moulded chimneys is the undersized hole in the top, giving the walls of the chimney an unrealistic 'thick and heavy' look when viewed from above. A suitably-sized twist drill twiddled between the fingers serves to open out this orifice to a more appropriate diameter.

Domes are less often affected by problems of outline than are chimneys, the

Hornby's old stager, the LMS Jinty, has a chimney that, as it comes, is not *quite* right. Reducing the height of the chimney top very slightly brings a big improvement; while I was at it, I took the funny pimple off the top of the dome.

bonnets, by and large, are similar to chimneys in the faults they exhibit - the too-thick top rim is by far the most common. A lot of people prefer to replace these with brass versions, either turned or lost wax cast, but I find a bit of filing often redeems the moulded original, as in the case of the Bachmann 93XX illustrated here. Don't forget, by the by, that after about 1930 the vast majority of GW safety valve casings were painted green, as here. The shiny brass beloved of modellers is nice, but unrealistic.

The main fault with most moulded-on GWR safety valve bonnets is an over-thick top rim, easily corrected by filing, as on the Mainline 43XX mogul illustrated.

A slightly more far reaching chimney modification is called for on the Replica / Mainline GWR 2251. This has a separate 'copper' chimney cap, fitted over the moulded plastic chimney barrel. Unfortunately, this gives a hole in the top of the chimney that is much too small, and puts the capuchon in the wrong place. I used the three sided scraper to ream out the hole, loosing the misplaced capuchon in the process. This was replaced with a piece of 1/2 mm square brass formed to a semi-circle and stuck in place with cyano.

most notable exception being the distinctly mammalian outline of the dome cover on the Mainline/Replica 57XX pannier tank.

Although this may well have been correct for an engine with a welded-in repair, most 57XXs had a dome of pure hemispherical outline; the difference is clearly shown when comparing the Replica model with my modified version. The change was simply effected by filing and sanding the dome to a more appropriate shape, and adding a retaining nut from 0.7mm wire cemented into a hole drilled in the centre of the top. GW-pattern safety valve

Correcting the oddly mammalian outline of the 57XX dome as rendered by Mainline - a touch of filing down, a hole, some brass wire and a careful trim with the Xuron snips.

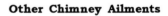

Even in GW days, these brass bonnets were often painted over. Replicating this feature makes models such as this Bachmann 93XX more authentic.

Other Chimney Ailments

A pet Rice hate and classic RTR giveaway is the chimney that is either solid almost to the top, or, worse still, has a very overscale fixing screw sticking out of it. In both cases, some careful drilling out is called for and, in the case of the screw, the devising of some less obtrusive way of retaining the body to the chassis. There are a few RTR locos, such as Dapol's J94 Austerity 0-6-0ST, which have loose chimneys retained by such a fixing screw. I stick the chimney in place and, once again, look for an alternative body fixing solution.

Two-Part Chimneys

Another common failing on RTR chimneys affects the two part moulded type used by several makers - Replica/Bachmann on the pannier, Airfix/Dapol with their Dean Goods and the new Bachmann 93XX Mogul are three examples. In these designs, the base of the chimney is moulded integrally with the smokebox top, but the barrel and rim are a separate moulding which is usually pegged into, and cemented to, the seating.

This is a great idea which can work well, but it has a couple of significant weaknesses. Firstly, faulty assembly can often give you a poor joint between the two halves of the chimney, which looks awful; it can also result in the upper portion of the thing being out of plumb. Secondly, it seems that the toolmakers often get things slightly wrong, with the result that the diameter of the barrel is the same as, or greater than, that of the seating. As on the real engine, the barrel fits *inside* the seating - this obviously looks wrong, and needs correcting.

The answer in both cases is to carefully saw the two parts of the chimney apart with the razor saw. The mating surfaces are then carefully sanded flat - we don't want to lose any significant height, so keep this sanding to a minimum. If the barrel diameter is OK, the two halves are rejoined using liquid cement. If, however, the barrel is too fat, as on the Dean Goods and 93XX, then the barrel is secured on a mandrel by the simple dodge of drilling it out from the top with a twist drill a mite larger than the moulded hole. The chimney should sit tight on the drill, which is then chucked in a handbrace clamped in the vice. The chimney can now be rotated slowly while a flat needle file and a 320 grit wet and dry flat rubbing stick are used to 'turn it down' a bit until the diameter is *slightly* less than that of the seating. I always check

the chimney are then reunited as already described. The drilling out part of the process is frequently needed whether or not the chimney is to be 'turned', as this type of moulding seems more prone than most to an undersized top orifice. Take particular care when cementing these chimneys back together that you get the upper part plumb in all planes; nothing looks worse than a Pisa-style smokestack, and you will have lost the benefit of the original locating peg when you sawed the thing apart in the first place.

Removing unwanted detail.

There are two reasons for loping off moulded detail from RTR locos; either because it's not appropriate to the particular engine you are modelling or, more likely, because you intend to replace it with something better. The three features I find myself most often removing in the latter catogory are moulded handrails - especially cab side grab rails - pipework and lamp irons.

The object of the exercise is to get rid of the moulded item with the minimum possible damage to the surrounding detail and to the underlying surface of the model. Masking tape will protect rivet or beading detail, but the real trick is to cut the unwanted part off cleanly enough to avoid the need for rubbing down. This comes down to the appropriate choice of cutting tool, usuaklly one of three : the the craft knife, the three sided scraper or the sharpened screwdriver. This last, used

Using a steel straight edge and sharpened screwdriver to remove moulded-on cab side rails from the 56XX.

neath it.

Any smoothing down of the surface needed once detail has been removed is best accomplished using the tip of the tapered 400-grits rubbing stick used with, soapy water. Any score marks can be filled with a wipe of cellulose knife putty, applied with a tiny scrap of cut up polybottle; leave this filler a fraction proud to allow for rubbing down. Any rivits that have gone AWOL during this process can be restored using the 'tiny' cube of Plastikard method, as illustrated in the photograph.

Basic redetailing.

At this point, we have reached the 'low ebb' so far as a basic body rework is concerned. Having started with a pretty presentable complete model, we are now reduced to a bare moulding or mouldings, rather scraped around and scrappy-looking, sans fittings, sans detail, probably sans quite a bit of paint, and certainly sans charisma. Don't, whatever you do, put the model next to an untouched specimen at this stage! Much better to press on straight away with the rebuilding work. The matter of finding, fettling, fabricating and fitting details is covered in detail in chapter 5, so for the moment I'm going to confine myself to describing the general sequence of redetailing, together with a few words on the simple basic additions that are rather more structural than superficial.

Handrails

While the actual mechanics of making up and fitting handrails figure large in the detailing chapter, there are a few general points to make. The first is that, for replacement handrails to constitute an improvement, they have got to be consistent, both with the rest of the handrails already on the loco, and with the general standard applying across the loco stud. There's no point in fitting super-fine handrails in dead-scale stanchions either side of the cab door if the main boiler rails are still the rather chunky (but still acceptable) efforts now factory-fitted to most RTR locos. Similarly, if you go to town with finescale rails on one loco, you've really got to write that into your standard for the whole stud, otherwise the

Impailing an oversize chimney barrel on a twist drill and sawing it free of the moulded base enables the diameter to be adjusted by 'turning', using a handbrace and a flat needle file. The two parts of the chimney are then cemented back together.

this by offering-up the two parts, rather than being clever on the measuring front.

Once the barrel is down to diameter and any rim-refining is completed (do that in the 'turning mode' while you're at it), the chimney is twisted off the drill and any further drilling out needed to get the correct internal diameter carried out. The two halves of

carefully, can take off a handrail or lamp iron from amid a veritable plethora of rivits withpout damaging any of them. The screwdriver needs to be seriously sharp, and must be used *gently*; once this, or any other tool, digs in, you've had it as far as an unmarked surface goes. To guide cutting tools, a steel ruler provides a usful reference edge as well as protecting detail be-one fine-railed loco will show the rest up. For myself, as indicated in Chapter 1, I link the type of handrails fitted to the degree of 'finescaling' I'm applying to the rest of the loco. Re-chassied EM or P4 conversions rate new rails; fine scale OO versions keep the factory items.

Other Basic Details

No main line locomotive ever ran anywhere on the railways of this country without displaying lamps or discs in an approved code. The brackets on which these indicators were mounted are, to me, a very fundamental item of locomotive anatomy. All my locos, in whatever scale or standard, get a set of lamp brackets. It is, furthermore, not that difficult to arrange removable lamps to go with them, and I would regard these as a great bonus in the quest for realistic operation. For me, one of the enormous benefits of modern high quality RTR locos, suitably modified, is that they enable one to assemble a reliable, balanced and realistic loco stud with which to equip a reasonably ambitious layout suited to *operation,* against a recent trend which has tended to produce exquisite but mummified museum pieces. Once again, the nuts and bolts of making and fitting lamp irons are meat for Chapter 5.

The other body mods that will usually need to be made on most RTR models may include the fitting of better buffers, the addition of full and decent bufferbeam detail and at least a cosmetic set of scale couplings, the replacement of moulded-on detail such as rainstrip and beadings that may have to be carved off in favour of something finer in Microstrip, and the glazing of cab windows and spectacles. Still at the cab end, don't forget that some sort of fall plate for tender locos will do away with that dreadful giveaway gap, while the matters of the coal and the crew must not be overlooked.

Closing the Gap

A modification I make on *all* RTR tender locos is to close up, often drastically, the hugely unrealistic gap between the loco and the tender. This is a product of lingering trainset mentality, which envisages curves of 15 inch radius or less. I wonder how many of the current generation of near-scale high quality RTR models get used on such trackwork? Not that many, I suspect. Surely it should be possible to accommodate the needs of the scale modeller with alternative tender coupling distances, as has been the practice in the USA for donkey's years? Even 24 inch radius curves allow a considerable closing of this unsightly gap.

Fortunately, the widespread adoption of the Mainline-style inverted hook on the tender, locating behind the drag beam of the loco, has eased the prob-

lem of adjusting the coupling gap. Adding packing inside the drag beam where the hook bears enables one to bring the tender in closer by controlled and incremental amounts. A piece of 40thou. Plastikard closes up the gap by about 1mm; I often end up with some 100thou. of packing here, to reduce the loco to tender distance by about half. This still gives enough clearance - around 4mm - to enable a loco to negotiate curves of around 24 inches radius; Peco short turnouts, for instance. There's almost always enough room between the back of the drag beam and the rear of the chassis for 2mm of packing before you start to run into problems with entering the hook into the remaining gap. If necessary, I file a bit off the front edge of the hook.

You don't want a lot of slack in loco to tender couplings, as that gives rise to unrealistic sloppiness in running between loco and tender. When reversing, real locos don't move a scale eighteen inches or more before the tender stirs from rest! Reducing such sloppiness is especially important on tender drive locos, and I touch on the business of shortening these rather more functional drawbars in chapter 6.

Don't Forget the Fall-Plate...

Even the smaller gap that results from the above operations will, however, still leave something to be desired in the realism department. ASLEF would, one imagines, have had something to say about a gurt great hole into which their members would inevitably fall from time to time, with results that don't bear contemplation. A fall-plate is the thing, either a pukka hinged job or,

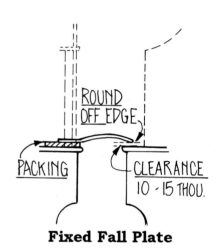

Fixed Fall Plate

more likely, a simple piece of 15thou. black Plastikard stuck to the rear of the loco footplate and packed beneath so that it clears the tender decking by 10thou. or so. A fall plate may need cut-outs to miss brake standards and other obstructions, while it should be shaped and dimensioned so that it does not impede the swing of the tender.

Details

The operations described in this chapter are, of course, only part of the story. While the correction of moulding faults, eradication of minor errors and general refining of the moulded body go a long way toward improving the authenticity and 'look' of an RTR loco, it's the detailing that really sets any model off, and that's a very big topic indeed. First, though, it is necessary to get to grips with the somewhat more drastic surgery involved in putting right the fundamental ills with which all too many RTR locos are still afflicted.

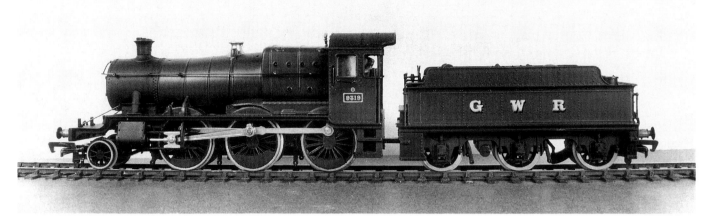

Send for the Loblolly Boys

So, for the next several pages, we're into the heavy stuff - amputations, transplants, organ removal, you know the sort of thing; the bits they only hint at on TV hospital soap operas. So, for now, it's time to scrub up, don the green gown, and send for the loblolly boys.

(For those of you who missed out on your *Hornblower*, these unlikely-sounding characters were the surgeon's mates aboard the ships of Nelson's navy; their job was to hold down the unfortunate victims while the surgeon set to with knives and bone-saws).

Above : As it comes out of the box, Bachmanns 93XX mogul has a monstrous chasam between loco and tender - in common with many other RTR locos. Why this should be so is beyond me, and closing the gap to somewhere near the appropriate distance is a priority.

Below : Here is the 93XX after being got at; the loco to tender gap has been halved, and a fixed fall plate installed as in the diagram. The moulded cab and tender handrails have been replaced with wire, to the considerable benefit of the models appearence. A couple of further improvements are still called for - the removal of that prominent mould part-line on the tender vacuum reservoir, and the provision of the tender to loco water hoses. Some better cab window glazing wouldn't go amiss, either.

SERIOUS SURGERY

Bachmann's 93XX mogul, as it comes, has a number of faults. Most galling of these is the combination of a wrongly placed footplate drop at the front, combined with undersized cylinders. Cut-and-shut was needed to correct the fore end of this loco.

There are two main reasons for performing major surgery on an RTR loco: to correct a fundamental fault, or to turn it into something other than what its makers intended it should be. The first of these reasons is pretty self-explanatory, and should, hopefully, be necessary on fewer and fewer occasions as the RTR makers advance their quality - and turn their backs on the sort of production expedient or 'trainset mentality' compromises that have marred so many mass market models in the past. The second reason, sometimes termed 'modelbashing', also seems to have gone out of favour somewhat, at least on this side of the Atlantic. This, I suspect, is due to the greater choice of models currently available, and the ever-increasing standard of authenticity throughout the hobby - a standard that will no longer accept a 'near enough' rehash as a satisfactory model. The days when you could bung a brass safety valve and a copper capped chimney on a Triang 'Jinty', paint it green with 'GWR' on the side, and reckon you'd got yourself a loco 'modelled after an absorbed Welsh class' are long gone.

Deciding whether or not it's worth attempting a major surgical reordering of an RTR loco body depends on a number of factors, of which the most important are the likely effectiveness of the modifications, and the difficulty of carrying them out. With enough fiddling about it would, I suppose, be possible to rectify almost any error on a moulded plastic body, given the facility with which the material can be cut, added to and joined. But in going very far down this road, you very soon reach the point where you might as well scratchbuild the thing in the first place, so complex can the process become. So, for instance, I would elect to live with the slightly over-wide firebox of Bachmann's GWR 93XX Mogul, as any correction would be horrendously difficult to achieve, and comparatively negligible in the effect it would have on the appearance of the model. Cutting and rejoining the footplate to get the fore-end drop in the right place, however, is both much simpler to achieve, and has a much more obvious impact on the look of the loco. An operation like this is thus thoroughly worthwhile.

Other examples of worthwhile body alterations involving quite far-reaching surgery include the repositioning of splashers, or, in cases such as the Airfix/Dapol LMS 4F, their replacement by something nearer the correct size and shape; removal and replacement of smokebox doors and major boiler fittings; and that old favourite, the opening out of models in search of missing daylight beneath the boiler. Other alterations in the quest for authenticity can also call for some pretty nifty incisions; changing cab window configurations, cab spectacles or roof vents can be tricky, though it's quite possible to build an entirely new cab onto an RTR body if need be. There are even kits available for this sort of work, typified by the Alan Gibson round top cab conversion for the evergreen 57XX illustrated in this chapter.

The surgery needed to fit some of these modification kits, greatly popularised by Crownline, can also be quite tricky. However, while fiddling about with knife and file you can console yourself with the thought that at least the problem of replacing the lopped-off bits has been taken care of by somebody else! Another of the examples in this chapter, my reworking of Hornby's Bullied light Pacific, uses quite a few Crownline parts, all very straightforward work on the face of it. But even surgery on this simple, slab-sided body brings problems of access for the saws, and the need to preserve adjoining detail calls for delicate work with the scalpel. In a similar way, working on diesel locos can also be a headache. Altering grille types or locations, de-

27

Typical of the sort of modification kit made for RTR locos is this Haye Development cab conversion for the old Airfix 'Castle', which backdates it to the earlier 'Star'. This particular model was built by Tony White, and has aquired some rather nice replacement boiler fittings.

leting (or adding) steam heating boilers, access hatches and headcode boxes are all operations calling for some careful cutting and joining plus, like as not, some tricky work with the filler.

Fitting conversion parts can often call for quite tricky surgery, as demonstrated by the awkward cutting and patching needed to fit Crown Line etched 'long' smoke deflectors to a Hornby Bulleid Light Pacific.

Wart Removal

In the usual cussed way of things, some of the most awkward surgical propositions are among the most minor, but most frequently required, of operations. Possibly the worst is the removal (without scarring) of quite minor bits of locomotive anatomy, such as fittings that are not appropriate to the particular engine you're modelling. A classic case of this sort of problem is the top feed casing on that ubiquitous 57XX pannier. These prominent fittings were only applied to these locos on reboiling, which took place from 1942 onwards. Thus, all the many 57XX models - of whatever ostensible 'make' - running around in pre-war livery ('Great Western' lettering or GWR 'Shirtbutton' monogram) are quite incorrect. Indeed, so are more than a few post-war versions, as by no means all of these locos acquired the top feed boiler. Cutting off the offending item without making a real mess of the boiler top and damaging the tank fillers and other tank top detail is almost impossible. It would have been so much better if this top feed had been supplied as a separate component, to be fitted by the customer as required. This is what the US makers do with their diesel models, which usually come with a nice little packet of detail parts that enable you to tailor your model to almost any prototype version.

Surgical Techniques

Obviously, I can't describe and illustrate in detail every single operation that is possible on an RTR bodyshell, so I've concentrated on the basic techniques used, illustrated by some fairly typical examples. However, before making that famous first incision - so! - it is necessary to plan very carefully how you intend, not just to dissect the body, but also how you reckon to put it all back together again. I always

aim to make things fit as precisely as possible, rather than hoping for the best and relying on filler to disguise the gaps.

Cutting Up

Cutting is the essence of surgery, and we have four basic techniques at our disposal. Using the knife, we can either cut through plastic mouldings by making repeated passes, or we can score one or both surfaces, and snap. Generally speaking, both these approaches only work for straight cuts. There is one other use for the knife - shaving, where thin layers of material are sliced away from a surface or edge to adjust a fit or remove unwanted surface detail. The other main technique for cutting is to use a saw, either a rigid-backed hacksaw or razor saw or the fine, flexible (and fragile!) piercing saw. The rigid saw is, once again, limited to straight cuts, working down from an outside surface or edge. The piercing saw *can* be used in the same way, but its real role is in fretting out holes and other openings.

The piercing saw is most often used in conjunction with the third cutting implement, the drill. A very great deal of quite delicate cutting out can be accomplished on RTR bodies by drilling a series of variegated holes to remove unwanted material, as, for instance, in fretting out the injectors of the 57XX pannier on my two P4 versions.

These holes can be linked as required with the piercing saw, the knife, or by filing. Drills are often used in conjunction with needle files, and these form our fourth main method of cutting plastic mouldings. The fine tapered files and rifflers, especially, can take an initial drilled hole out to almost any desired shape.

I never use powered cutting tools such as abrasive discs, dental burrs or fine slitting saws on plastics. By and large, I find them too violent in their action, and hence too often uncontrollable in their effect. These moulding grade plastics are anyway too soft a material to be worked with rotating high speed cutters like these; the result is often overheating, with melting of the plastic material and binding of the tool the likely results. However, I do occasionally find a sharp dental burr chucked in a pin vice and rotated in the fingers a useful way of removing material from the inner edges of openings or in some otherwise inaccessible places.

When cutting up an RTR body for rejoining later, rather than simply removing unwanted material, I always aim to make the actual cuts as fine as possible, to allow the maximum leeway for fitting when it comes to sticking the parts of the model back together. To this end, I often find myself using a finer pitch piercing or razor saw blade than is perhaps ideal for plastic (conventional wisdom being that the softer the material being cut, the coarser the saw pitch used, to allow the cut material to clear the saw teeth easily). I find that, so long as you work carefully, lubricate the blade (with soap) and *never, ever* force the saw, then no problems arise.

Cleaning Up Cut Parts

Given care in the cutting, it shouldn't be necessary to do too much cleaning up of cut edges. Simple cutting rag or burrs are best scraped away with the edge of the blade of a sharp craft knife, as sanding cut plastic rarely gives a clean result - the dust tends to stay put due to electrostatic attraction. Where you do need to sand a mating face flat to make a good join with another part of the model, *always* use a sanding board and rub the model on it; *never* attack the model with a piece

When truing an edge, always rub the part on a file or sanding board laid flat on the bench.

of abrasive paper wrapped around your finger, for that way lie hollows and hillocks and other unhelpful bits of topography. Using a file to true up an edge is also not a good idea, as this type of filing is a skilled business. For most of us, the likely result is a surface or edge that's anything *but* true.

If you find (as you most certainly will) that, at the end of your sanding or filing operations, the abraded surface and its immediate surroundings are covered in a layer of dust which seems determined to stay put, you will need to resort to some sort of cleaning procedure. A brush moistened with the merest trace of Mek will pick up small quantities of such detritus, while a piece of sticky tape used tacky side down will remove larger accumulations. It's best to 'kill' the tape a bit by sticking it to a hard, smooth surface and peeling it off a few times (or use freezer tape spirited out of the kitchen) to avoid the chance of any adhesive contaminating the surface of the model, where it's the very devil to remove. (Lighter fuel, if the worst happens...) If you're doing a lot of carving around of a plastic body, you may find

that the whole thing becomes covered with plastic dust. In which case, a bath in warm, soapy water to which a bit of fabric conditioner has been added will both remove the dust and reduce the static charge on the plastic which attracts it.

Re-Joining

The first essential of the rebuilding phase of a dismembered RTR loco body is fit; if at all possible, you want to be in a position to put the thing together with precision, so that all the mating surfaces are in contact over the maximum area, and the requirement for gap-filling is minimised. If you can achieve this desirable state of affairs, the finished model will not only look better, but will also be far more robust. As with all good surgery, the aim is to restore the pre-cutting status quo, and

not to leave any visible scars.

Achieving a good fit between parts is a very fundamental modelling skill. Indeed, it is *the* skill on which scratch building, still generally regarded as the 'highest' form of modelmaking, is founded. As with so many things in life, there's no 'instant formula' to make a skilled fitter of you, but care, concentration and a light touch go a long way. The essence of fitting is constant trial and error, with the very frequent offering-up of the part being fitted to the rest of the job to which it must mate. Never, ever, kid yourself you'll do it by measurement, no matter how sophisticated the measuring implements you use. The man who can measure, cut, finish and fit to an exactness that would need to be expressed in several places of metric decimals is a better man than I, Gunga Din. But give me a part that's slightly too big, a fine sanding board and a couple of needle files, and I'll take off a smidgin here and a gnats whisker there until - Bingo! A fit.

That is the essence of fitting as we need to achieve it in the context of building up cut-about RTR loco bod-

ies. Wherever possible (and it almost always is possible), make the bit too big or the hole too small, and then finally and carefully adjust the pieces until they will just go together. There are quite a few aids to this delicate process, of which the most useful is the paper template. Say, for instance, you're faced with the need to make a patch to fill in some awkward hole in a body moulding left by the removal of some unwanted part - a 57XX top feed, perchance? Having trued the hole to the least awkward shape, place a scrap of typing paper over it, and make a rubbing with a soft 3B pencil, or , in my case, a wax crayon poached from No.2 daughter. This will give you an outline of the required patch. I cut this rudimentary template out with craft knife or scissors, and use it to produce a suitable Plastikard blank, with a reasonable 'finishing allowance', from which I can finish-fit the required patch.

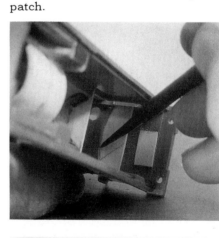

An acurate fit between parts makes joining a lot simpler; and this can call for some nifty fitting work on occasions - as here where a new section is being let into the cab rear of the Wrenn R1 body which forms the example in this chapter. The piece is cut oversize and offered up for scribing, shown in the first picture. Careful finishing to the scribed line results in a precise fit and a strong joint.

Making Joints

Moulded plastic loco bodies are produced in polystyrene, which is, of course, the same material as is used for making plastic kits as well as being rolled into sheet form as styrene sheet - 'Plastikard' or 'Evergreen' being the two most popular brands. The same solvents and glues will thus be effective on all three, and Mek-Pak liquid plastic cement is the usual choice for joining operations when rebuilding chopped-about RTR bodies. Being a solvent, it works by dissolving the plastic material of the mating surfaces in the joint, which re-harden when the solvent evaporates, producing, in effect, a solid welded joint. The strength of such a joint is dependent on the density and quality of this 'weld', which is at its greatest where the surfaces being joined are in total contact, hence the emphasis on an accurate fit.

If there is a gap to be filled, then the dissolved plastic is, effectively, spread thinner in filling the space between the parts. This makes for a weaker joint, but you can help to overcome this by introducing a bit more plastic into the equation. There are two ways of doing this; you can either make the join with a paste-type plastic cement rather than the liquid solvent, or you can add finely divided plastic to the solvent in the gap. The former option, using the sort of tube plastic cement with which we all used to ruin two shilling Airfix aeroplane kits, is a bit of a last resort, used only where the gap is wide; it's awfully difficult to control this cement, which has a nasty habit of squeezing out of the joint and getting where it's not wanted.

Much better is to use the liquid solvent, and to add some extra plastic. This is an abundant resource wherever plastic is being filed or sanded - that same dust which can be such a nuisance when working plastic can be equally useful when joining it. Dip a small brush in the solvent, pick up a little dust from the sanding board, and introduce the resulting sludge into the open joint from the unseen side, adding more solvent as necessary to help the plastic slurry penetrate the crack. A joint filled like this is a great deal stronger than the 'thin' version described above.

Of course, it's often possible to reinforce joints with a patch or fillet on an unseen face, and this should be done wherever practicable. However, do keep checking the fit of the body on its chassis if you're putting these patches on the inside of the moulding; some of these RTR bodies, especially the steam engines, are a *very* tight fit over their mechanisms, and even a piece of 10thou. Plastikard in the wrong place can result in a body that will no longer fit onto its chassis. Here speaks the voice of one who has found out the hard way!

Heat Welding

As well as the 'chemical welding' just described, it is occasionally possible to unite parts or reinforce a solvent-made joint by physically melting and flowing the plastic with the tip of the small soldering iron used for melting in detail. This can work quite well on mouldings of reasonable thickness -

say, 1.5mm or more, but is decidedly dodgy on thin material. It can also affect the factory finish, so if you're intent on preserving paint, give this technique a miss.

The need for patching is the most frequent operation in rebuilding chopped-around RTR loco bodies. Cutting out an unrealistic set of solid 'boiler skirts' - as on the Wrenn R1 used as the main illustration in this chapter - is a typical fretwork and patch modification, the patch in this case being the provision of the bottom portion of the boiler. Other patches and let-in pieces include the rebuilding of the footplate around relocated splashers, as on the R1 and 4F, the blocking-in of unwanted window or grille openings, as on several diesels, and the reworking of the front end of the airsmoothed casing of the Bulleid Pacific, ready for the fitting of overlaid etched smoke deflectors.

Cutting and Shutting Operations

At their most drastic, these operations involve the complete cutting apart of a whole body moulding, and the rejoining of the parts either in a different order, or as a means of combining parts of two or more body mouldings to make an entirely new model. This is a technique often used by American modellers to produce variations on their diesel prototypes, where the same basic locomotive design can appear in a great many guises. By combining, say, the 'short hood' from model A with the cab from model B and the 'long hood' from model C with the frame from something else and a couple of pilots (bufferbeams without buffers) lurking in the scrapbox form some previous butchery, your dedicated US modeller can come up with a model of an unusual or one-off prototype.

Given the very different nature of the British prototype, both steam and die-

sel, such far-reaching and complex surgery isn't called for very often. This isn't to say there isn't scope, as I'm sure there are some unexplored possibilities out there. Where the same type of technique *is* relevant is on the rather smaller scale needed to correct basic dimensional errors. A good example is the moving of the wrongly-placed front footplate drop of the Bachmann 93XX, which entails cutting the footplate of the model into three pieces, which are then re-assembled in a different order to correct the error. Similarly drastic surgery made it possible to remove the puzzling (why *did* they do it?) excess length from the smokebox of Hornby's 'Albert Hall'.

Specific Procedures

Having discussed in general terms the approaches and techniques available to the dedicated loco body butcher, it would now seem appropriate to look at a few specific cases where these procedures have been used to improve RTR bodies. The main example is the old Hornby - Dublo ex-SECR 'R1' 0-6-0T (not, I hasten to add, the highly collectable original Dublo example, but a new Wrenn body in an alarming shade of pink, purchased as a spare from Dapol), which has a good selection of classic RTR compromises about its anatomy.

There are, to start with, two unprototypical motor clearance bulges in the rear of the firebox, no daylight under the boiler, a totally inaccurate cabfront, with slots rather than the

The Wrenn - nee Hornby Dublo - R1 0-6-0T incorporates a lot of errors and compromises that are tricky to correct - especially when, as here, the body is to be fitted to a new scale chassis. Note, for instance the displacement of the leading splasher in relation to the driving wheel; the *wheel* is in the right place.

correct circular cab spectacles, and some very low-relief steps. Less obvious (and far trickier to correct) is an error in the front splasher/sandbox; the splasher is too far aft, but the sandbox (integral with the smokebox front) is in the right place. The problem is thus to cut the splasher free of the sandbox and footplate with minimal damage, removing the daylight-obstructing boiler skirt in the process. The sandbox then has to be cut free of the smokebox, and modified to allow the splasher to move forward by around 2mm, and the whole lot reassembled and made good, a process that also calls for the provision of a boiler bottom. The solution to this fiendish (but, for once, non-Chinese) puzzle appears over the page....

Compared with this very particular piece of awkwardness, the other shortcomings of the R1 body seem trivial. The remaining surgery - the provision of a corrected cab front and firebox rear, the removal and replacement of the steps, the refining of the edges to the cab openings and the opening up of the bunker for a proper coal load - is pretty straightforward. Taken together with the usual need for scale handrails, metal strip lamp irons, a decent set of bufferbeam fittings, a full cab interior and full-relief pipework - not to mention a better steam reverser and a decent coal load - the rest of the conversion is almost a cinch! I should perhaps point out at this stage that the R1 - a very vintage piece of plastic moulding dating from 1959 - was picked as an example primarily *because* it exhibited such a wonderful selection of challenges, although the moulding does incorporate some delightful detail touches. Just to make life that little bit more interesting, the R1 was selected to go the whole finescale hog, the reworked body sitting on a 'Branchlines' etched chassis fitted with a DS10 motor, Ultrascale 50:1 gears and Ultrascale P4 wheels.

Fretting Out

The main surgical procedure needed when undertaking far-reaching modifications such as those applied to the R1 is the fretting-out of openings to remove unwanted material, or to separate individual parts for moving or replacement. As the sequence of photographs shows, this process starts with the drilling of a series of holes on waste areas of the moulding, to allow the blade of the piercing saw to be entered or turned. The piercing saw is fitted with a fairly fine blade (I used an M3/0) with the teeth of the blade pointing back towards the saw handle. The blade, secured at the handle end, is then threaded through the most appropriate hole, the free end then being clamped and the blade tensioned. This tensioning is usually best achieved by pushing the nose of the saw against the front of the bench or some other immovable object while the clamping screw is tightened. The blade is now lubricated with a drop of washing up liquid, and the unwanted portion of the body moulding is then cut away by sawing around the outline on the waste side of the required finished line. You may find you can't cut the whole outline in one hit - never try and work the

Fretting out - basically a matter of joining up a few holes with the piercing saw. Drill the holes at all the corners, then link them with saw cuts; to get the saw in, cutting has to be done at quite a shallow angle - lubricate the blade well with washing up liquid.

saw awkwardly, as that only results in busted blades. If necessary (and it usually is, in my experience) unclamp and withdraw the blade for re-threading in a hole giving a better working direction of cut.

The alternative to sawing out a waste area, such as the unprototypical 'boiler skirt' of the R1, is to carry on with the drill, making a series of holes in the waste material, holes which can then be linked up with the Xuron snips, a heavy craft knife, or by filing. The final finishing to shape and outline of the resulting opening is always a matter of filing anyway, so it's just a case of extending this process back a bit. With very large areas of waste to remove, it's probably best to drill a series of smallish holes around the outline, postage stamp perforation style, and then cut or break the centre away. For small areas, several largish holes, big enough to take the tip of a square section or triangular tapered needle file - plus smaller holes in corners and close to edges - provide the quickest and most efficient approach.

Cutting out the R1s front splashers and sandboxes, shortening them and refitting them was just about as tricky an operation as you are likely to come across when modifying RTR bodies. The first cuts, made with the piercing saw, were started from a hole drilled through the footplate at the front edge of the splasher. Entering the saw through this hole enabled me to cut along the base of the splasher, and also to part the front of the sandbox from the smokebox wing plate. The final cut could then be made with the razor saw, separating the sandbox top from the smokebox. The razor saw was also used to shorten the severed splasher at the front end; when refitted to the loco, the splasher and wheel centres now lined up.

Removing Individual Components

When it comes to parting something specific, such as a splasher or sandbox, from the rest of the body moulding, then the piercing saw is the only way in 99% of cases. Unless you can work from a waste area or pre-cut opening, the trick here is to drill only the smallest size hole that will accept the sawblade at saw entry and turning points. The part is then cut away by *carefully* sawing around the outline, trying always to err on the waste side of the line if there is one. Piercing saws are cussed sort of things, and will wander off in unpremeditated directions at the drop of a hat. Keep the blade well lubricated, and go very slowly. You may also find that a scribed line along the outline required will stop the saw from meandering off into the unknown. These techniques are illustrated, as far as is practicable without video, in the picture sequences.

With care, it is possible to cut parts away very accurately, and with a minimal loss of material in the width of the sawcut. A further example of this sort of operation is the removal of the radiator shutter grilles of my Alco RS11 diesel, which needed to be transposed side-for-side to get the activating motor in the right place for the particular engine I was modelling. I managed to cut these free accurately enough to get

a more or less exact fit when each grille was reinserted in the opposite side of the hood. A backing patch on the inside of the moulding and the merest trace of filler completed the job. It wasn't possible to get *quite* such a good fit on the R1's splashers, but even here, using a fine blade and plenty of care, I was able to reduce the need for filling to a minimum.

When it came to cutting out the R1 cab front for replacement, you'll note that I gave myself an easier fitting job by electing to cut square across the top of the opening, rather than following the curve of the cab roof. This made it comparatively easy to make and fit the correction patch with the new cab spectacles, and I considered that I could hide the resulting join well enough, although theoretically this would have been easier had it followed the outline of the cab roof. As part of the same operation, the two unprototypical bulges on the firebox were cut away and replaced with sections of pre-curved 40thou. Plastikard let in, reinforced with backing patches inside the boiler. Fortunately the new chassis, with the DS10 motor driving the rear axle, permitted this remedy. Retaining the original chassis without modification would mitigate against any correction of this unfortunate production compromise.

Other Surgical Removals

Cutting away dummy moulded coal loads is another typical fretting operation. The rest of the cutting away on this model, however, involved taking detail or components off a surface, rather than out of the thickness of the main moulding. Thus, the moulded-on handrails, pipework and lamp irons were removed with a craft knife, scraper and sharpened screwdriver as already described. Also removed in this instance were some moulded-on rear bunker lamp irons, the clack valves and tank fillers, and the steam reverser. The unsatisfactory steps were cut off with the razor saw, and the over-thick edges of the cab openings mitred off with the scraper. All the cut edges were cleaned up with the needle files and fine (400 grit) wet and dry paper and rubbing sticks, used wet. With all this surgery completed, the very sorry-looking body shell was ready for rebuilding.

Other Major Surgery

Although in some ways more drastic than the sort of operations performed on the hapless R1, the business of cutting a body moulding apart completely for major substitution or for combining with other mouldings or conversion kit components can often

Removing and refitting diesel grilles is another operation calling for accurate cutting. To get the operating motor housing at the right end of the grille on this diesel, I swoped the identical component side for side reversing the grille layout. A cut was made up each side using the razor saw; the top of the grille was parted by scoring with a craft knife and snapping out. The grilles were then refitted in their new locations, with plastikard backings inside the body mouldings to reinforce the joints. The gap resulting from the width of the saw cuts was taken up with some fine Microstrips. Very little finish filling was required.

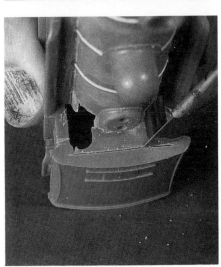

Another similar operation is the replacement of the R1s badly compromised cab front with a proper spectacle plate. The razor saw parted the cab front from the boiler, and the craft knife was used to score the top of the opening for snapping out. The resulting hole was trued up with files, enabling a simple rectangular patch to be let in. Finally, this was drilled and reamed to give correctly sized and located cab spectacles.

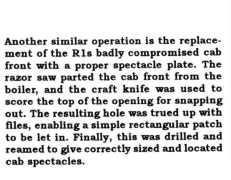

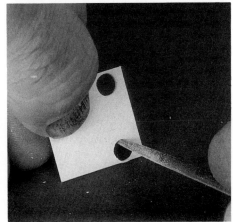

be more straightforward than the tricky business of fretting-out holes or bits. The example here is a Replica 57XX body, being cut to receive the Alan Gibson (ex-M&L) cast cab and bunker conversion that gives an engine of the later 8750 batch. (The objective in this case was to produce a P4 model of No.3635 with Perseverance chassis, for my Cornish china clay branch.) Such an operation can be performed on the standard OO version with equal facility.

The implement in this case is the X-Acto razor saw, with the deeper type of blade that enables you to cut virtually right through an RTR body in one

This is the other common surgical requirement, and is frequently not as easy as it might seem. Simply sawing off a chimney or dome down to the base is simple enough; it's getting rid of the seating moulded on to the boiler or smokebox top without damaging or destroying rivet or boiler band detail that's the real problem. Again, sharp cutting tools used as accurately as possible are to be preferred to files or abrasives, which tend to be rather less selective in what they remove.

The basic procedure is to cut the offending fitting as close to the boiler top

better to fret out the piece of the boiler top on which the fitting is mounted, and then make good the resulting hole. This isn't easy in itself, but it's the lesser of two evils.

Stitching Up

The rebuilding of the much cut-about R1 encompasses just about every aspect of the re-assembly and making good process, so it can continue to serve as our main example. The first, and trickiest, job was to reinstate the splashers and sandboxes, fit a boiler bottom, and make good the footplate. The sandboxes had been cut free of the

Cutting up the Replica 57XX body to receive the Alan Gibson round top cab conversion calls for some pretty deep cuts. The bunker is first removed by cutting horizontally through its retaining tabs. The cab front is then parted from the tanks by sawing right down to footplate level using the deep bladed Exacto Razor Saw; even this wouldn't *quite* reach, so the cut was completed with the piercing saw. The bottom of the cab sides were separated from the footplate by cutting with the saw from the outside, and the knife from the inside. End result - a 57XX ready for its new rear end.

swipe.

To modify the 57XX body for its new cast cab, it is necessary to make some pretty accurate cuts, as the rear of the bunker is retained, and mated to the new cabsides, the joint following the similar joint on the prototype. After stripping off the handrails of the model, and removing the cab roof by running a sharp craft knife around the joint with the cabsides, the two vertical cuts are made using the razor saw. Rather than trying to keep the bunker rear attached to the footplate as suggested in the instructions, I simply ran the razor saw across the back of the loco immediately above the footplate, and then at an angle along each side. The coal load was also done away with at the same time, saving only the handbrake cover.

Surgery was completed by cleaning up the cut edges with a fine flat needle file and the fine sanding board.

as can be achieved without prejudicing surrounding detail. The residue is then removed with a sharp cutting tool, usually the three sided scraper. Go gently, using the tool lightly and not attempting to take off too much material at once.

Only when as much of the errant fitting as is humanly possible has been carefully carved away do I consider using abrasives, and then it's only a fine needle file or riffler, followed by the fine 400 grit rubbing stick used, as usual, 'wet'. A few pieces of masking tape stuck over vulnerable detail will help protect it, but at the end of the day the loss of a few rivets when parting a chimney from a smokebox top is almost inevitable. Reinstate them with the Plastikard cube method described in the next chapter. Occasionally, where you just can't get at the offending fitting with either saws or scraper - as with that 57xx top feed - it may be

smokebox wing plate at the front end, and the boxes were now shortened by the required amount - around 1.5mm - to bring them into the right relationship with the wheels and the smokebox. The drop from sandbox top to splasher top should coincide with the rear edge of the smokebox, and not sit some 2mm aft of that point, as Dublo have it. (Why? Given that this model had a 'dedicated' chassis, this odd compromise seems pointless, as do so many of them).

The sandboxes were carefully filed to get a really good fit at the fore end, where the joint lies just behind the vertical beading. They were then cemented in place with Daywat Poly, which gives the strongest bond to this particular grade of styrene. The joint below the footplate was reinforced with fillets of 10thou. Microstrip behind the footplate angles, and by running epoxy resin into the inside of the sandbox/

Ugh! Mainline's 43XX mogul has a horrible chimney, so it's out with the razor saw and a quick cut through as close to the smokebox as practicable. The remains are then carefully carved away with the three sided scraper, and the result smoothed down with the fine rubbing stick to give a clear seating for the new cast chimney.

wing plate joint. The joint with the smokebox received the solvent plus plastic dust treatment to get a good weld. This was all left to set off hard overnight. The rest of the making good could then be finished off.

There was now a 2mm gap between the rear of the splasher and the footplate in front of the tank front. Rather than try and let in a little tiny piece of Plastikard, I cut the footplate back to the tankfront in line with the splasher front, and made a patch of 50thou. to fit this much larger opening. The patch was reinforced with a further piece of 10thou. Plastikard below the footplate. The residual gaps were all gratifyingly tiny, and were filled with cellulose knife stopping thinned with Mek-Pak and brushed into place. (Don't use your best paintbrush for this job - it won't be your best brush afterwards if you do!).

Boiler Patching

The next job - a very common one - was to make a bottom section for the boiler to continue its form in the areas previously hidden by the unprototypical vertical 'boiler skirts' that used to be a very common feature on many older RTR locos. It is also

a job often called for when a pancake motor mechanism, frequently incorporating part of the loco boiler integrally cast as a ballast weight, is replaced by an etched brass finescale chassis, as on the Replica 57XX and 2251, among others.

The provision of the missing boiler bottom in these cases can be quite a tricky little matter, as any patch will need to be pre-formed to the correct radius to match the boiler before fitting. I make these patches out of fairly thick Plastikard - 40 or 50thou. - which has quite a lot of 'spring', and doesn't take kindly to be asked to follow smallish radii. My approach is to cut the material to the correct *length*, but to leave plenty of excess on the width. The plastic is then taped or rubber-banded to a piece of dowelling several sizes smaller in radius than the desired finished result, and immersed in very hot (boiling if possible) water for a few minutes. This usually does the trick, and should result in a a nicely curved piece of Plastikard that, even allowing for the inevitable 'spring-back', should be somewhere near the right curvature to match the boiler. The edges can then be carefully trimmed back for a fit into the moulded boiler, finishing by bevelling the mating surfaces with a file as

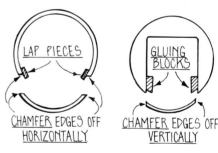

Boiler Bottoms

in the diagram. I have found that you don't need to be spot-on with the radius of curvature - as long as it's somewhere near right it'll look OK.

Fixing such a boiler bottom in place is no sinecure either. A lot depends on the shape of the hole you're trying to fit it into. If, as with the R1, it has vertical sides, then you're laughing, as it's a simple matter to weld a couple of pieces of 60thou. square Microstrip in place as stops to set the patch at the right height to match the outside face of the moulding. Where the boiler is truly hollow, as on the 2251, then it's not so easy. I try cutting a couple of formers of appropriate radius to weld into the boiler to support the patch. This is, I'm afraid, another case of trial and error, although with a taper boiler like the 2251's, at least your former should fit *somewhere* along the taper! I cut these circular formers from 40thou. Plastikard sheet using a pair of sharp dividers to scribe the sheet.

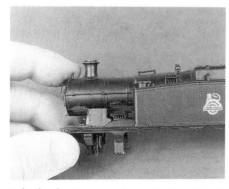

A boiler bottom patch in 20 thou black plastikard being fitted to the 56XX. As in the diagram, a pair of lap pieces have been cemented to the boiler ready to receive the patch. Once the joint has hardened, it can be filled and sanded to give a smooth and continuous surface to the boiler.

Either keep going until you break through, or cut out a square just containing the circle, snap of the corners, and clean up with wet and dry paper.

Flat Patches

These are generally a lot easier to make and fit than the curved variety, and are produced in plastic sheet of a thickness as near equal to the thickness of the mouldings as is possible. Obviously, a flush joint on the outer face is the thing that matters, and it may often pay to make your patch a shade *too* thick, sanding down the proud portion once it is secured in place. Wherever possible, reinforce flat patch joints with fillets or other patches of thin (10thou., usually) material on the in-

side of the body. As always, go for an accurate fit by making the piece that has to be let in oversize, carefully finish-filing it to final size. Having to do a lot of filling around a flat patch means you missed the mark in this respect; if you do end up with wide or unsightly gaps, it's always worth considering going for 'take two' rather than trying to fill some gaping chasm.

Additions

It is quite often necessary to make some quite fundamental structural additions to RTR bodies, particularly where they are being re-chassied. Cab floors, for instance, are often sacrificed

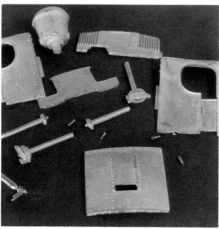

to the spatial needs of the mechanism. With a well planned replacement chassis, often fitted with a far more compact motor than the RTR original, it is often possible (and always desirable) to reinstate these - a load of daylight showing where the driver is supposed to stand is never all that convincing, I find. Where you're going one stage further and adding cab interior detail - as on both the R1 and the 57XX featuring in this chapter - then it will often pay to build up this cab floor as a sub-assembly complete with boiler backhead, crew and other footplate fittings. When you fix this to the rest of the loco depends on whether or not the model features a removable cab roof.

A pretty major addition - the substitute round top cab for the 57XX pannier tank. These cast parts, from Alan Gibson, fit beautifully, and mate with the original bunker rear. The castings were glued to the plastic body with a mixture of Cyano - to tack thigs in place - and Araldite. The end result is an accurate cab that blends well with the moulded body; when painted it's a job to spot the joins.

Even if the cab floor can't be in quite the right place, as on my converted Mainline J72, an aptly placed piece of Plastikard looks a lot more convincing then unadulterated daylight showing through.

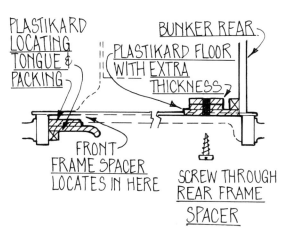

PLASTIKARD LOCATING TONGUE & PACKING

BUNKER REAR

PLASTIKARD FLOOR WITH EXTRA THICKNESS

FRONT FRAME SPACER LOCATES IN HERE

SCREW THROUGH REAR FRAME SPACER

Body Mountings

If this is fixed, don't install your cab interior until the model is more or less complete - usually at the painting stage.

Body Mountings

On some locos - the R1 included - it is necessary to provide at least a partial floor to the bunker to act as a 'landing' for one end of the chassis, the original RTR loco in this case relying on an unsightly rear tongue that protruded through the bunker back. A floor of this type may also need to incorporate a body fixing, which in the case of the R1 was a small self-tapping screw into the dummy floor. A slightly undersized hole and a couple of extra thicknesses of Plastikard welded onto the top of this piece of floor will give this fixing screw extra 'bite'. The front of the chassis was held by a locating tongue, built up from more Plastikard as in the diagram. It's not always possible to engineer such nice, solid body mountings, especially on locos originally held together by the coupling screws. On quite a few of my RTR conversions, the body is held on by no more than a tight fit on the chassis, or by an appropriately sized blob of Blu-Tak fore and aft. 'Orrid, but surprisingly effective.

After the Stitches Come Out...

With the moulded body back in one piece and the wounds, as far as possible, healed with filler and careful sanding, it's time to get onto the really enjoyable part of the business - detailing. From now on, not even the most squeamish will find anything to baulk at.

Below : The carved about R1 now sits happily on its Branchlines etched chassis, built by Frank Watts. Boiler bands in Plastikard and Microstrip have already been added, and the body is now ready to receive its new detail.

Chapter Five

Detailing

My old 14XX, rebuilt from an early Airfix example, has been extensively redetailed using the techniques described in this chapter.

Detailing of RTR locos comes into two categories: replacing unsatisfactory detail that was on the loco when you bought it, and adding things that the makers left off. Quite often, the two will overlap, as when original RTR handrails are replaced by finer wire and turned stanchions, with additional rails added using the same components. I have a very definite approach to the provision of all the principal types of loco detail, and in the interests of consistency (an interest which, remember, hold in the highest regard) I find that it pays to use the same techniques and components wherever possible. So, without further preamble, let's consider the main types of detail fitting we have to provide, starting with that universal bete noir, handrails.

Handrails

Nothing makes or breaks the detailing on a model loco more than the fineness and quality of the handrails. That's as true of my favourite Yankee diesels as it is of traditional Bulldog steamers, so it's worthwhile taking the time and trouble needed to get this feature right. It's something I always pay great attention to when comparing erstwhile 'to be improved' models with prototype photos. However, it's also important to bear in mind that making handrails, particularly of the sort that go along one side of the boiler, up over the smokebox front, and back down the other side, is none too easy. Before you remove and junk some slightly chunky but otherwise satisfactory factory-fitted rails, try making the replacements. Then compare your efforts with the originals, and be honest with yourself about which is the bet-

ter set!

On most RTR loco bodies that are subjected to any sort of workover, one of the greatest single detailing jobs is the provision of wire handrails to replace carved-off moulded versions. Grab iron handrails - that is, those that are simply staple-shaped bent metal - are amongst the details that I fit by 'melting in', a technique described in a page or two. If, however, I need to fit 'proper' handrails using turned stanchions (the things that several generations of modellers have referred to as 'handrail knobs'), then it's a matter of drilling some holes in the correct locations, and fitting the appropriate wire and stanchions.

Unfortunately, laying hands on the appropriate stanchions may not be too easy, as for the sake of consistency they will need to match the stanchions of any existing factory-fitted handrails as closely as possible. Obviously, the ideal solution will be to obtain some identical stanchions as a spare from the maker of your RTR loco, but that's often impossible. So I'm afraid that it's usually a case of rummaging around the bits stand at your local model shop or trying the various specialists at exhibitions, in search of something with the right visual 'weight'. This matching problem is often the reason that I sometimes end up replacing *all* the handrails on an RTR loco, even where the factory-fitted rails are otherwise satisfactory. If you do hoick off any RTR handrails, never, but *never,* throw them away. Salt them down in the junkbox against the day when you need a few matching stanchions for some other RTR conversion. The cabside handrails on my OO 57XX, for instance, used stanchions salvaged from the handrails of the P4 version,

which, in keeping with its finescale aspirations, had slimmer rails in scale size knobs.

Fitting Handrails

When drilling holes to take the shanks of handrail stanchions - or any other fitting with a similar shank or peg fitting, if it comes to it - it always pays to drill the mounting hole in the plastic body undersize. If you then carefully open out the hole with your taper broach until the shank will just enter the *front* of the hole (which is now slightly tapered, due to the action of the broach), then the stanchion can be pushed home to make a nice tight fit in the hole. If you find that the stanchion is sticking out a bit too much from the surface of the body and holding the rail too far off the loco, you can countersink the stanchion holes a trifle to set them back a bit.

The best method of securing turned stanchions in a moulded plastic body depends on several factors. If you can get at the inside of the body at the stanchion location, and the shank of the stanchion is long enough to come through the thickness of the moulding, then it's a simple matter to fix the turning with a drop of epoxy over the tail where it sticks through the body moulding. If the tail is too short to allow of this, then a tiny drop of cyano in the hole before the stanchion is entered will serve - but make sure that you've got the alignment spot-on before you push the stanchion home, as once the cyano has gone off, that is it. The third method is simply to broach out the hole sufficiently undersize for the turning to make a good tight fit when you push it home.

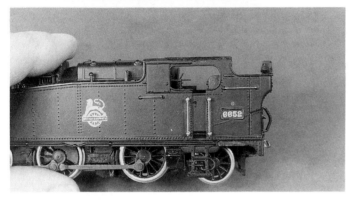

Fitting new cab side rails - the stanchions are located in the holes, and the wire threaded through and secured with Cyano. The surplus wire is then snipped off, resulting in a neat pair of matched cab side handrails.

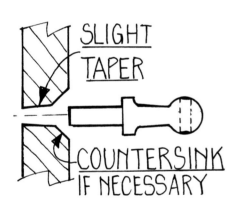

Fixing Handrail Stanchions

It's important to match as closely as possible the stanchions used for additional handrails with the factory-fitted items. If you can't salvage enough from other modelling projects, I've found that the turned brass knobs produced by Ferndale Forge are a good match. You should be able to get these through your local model shop.

Making Handrails

Providing the actual rail is simply a matter of selecting some wire of the appropriate diameter. This wants to be straight-drawn and fairly hard (although not so hard, as with piano wire, that it won't bend and takes nibbles out of the cutting edge of your wire snips). I use either hard brass wire or nickel silver - see sources listed in the index. Most finescale turned handrail stanchions are designed to take 0.45mm diameter wire, which scales out at just under one and a half inches diameter, accurate for the majority of full size rails. The staple-type grabs not carried in stanchions are often a bit smaller than this, being about one inch in diameter, and for these the smaller 0.33mm wire is absolutely spot-on.

Forming and fitting handrail wire can be quite tricky, although if you've got a set of factory handrails to copy you can save yourself a lot of trial and error. Look out, though, if your new stanchions are substantially shorter than the factory originals, as this will 'move' the bending points for one piece boiler rails slightly. If you are faced with the need to form a continuous rail from scratch, I find that it's best to start at the knob in the top middle of the smokebox front, and work out both ways. Once you've got the profile of the rail over the smokebox door and the two corner bends right, the rest is simple. Well, simple-ish. Don't forget to thread the smokebox front knob or knobs on *before* you make those cor-

ner bends...

Cabside handrails in stanchions are sometimes made up off the loco, the stanchions being secured to the wire at the correct spacing with a tiny drop of solder or cyano. A simple paper template, or even a jig consisting of a couple of holes in a scrap of Plastikard, can help to produce matched sets of cabside rails, which look awful if they don't match accurately. Templates are also useful for forming grabs, which are then melted into place using my melt-in jig and the small 15W iron, of which more in a moment.

Handrail Blackening

I have already expressed my preference for chemically blackened handrails, so naturally I treat all the

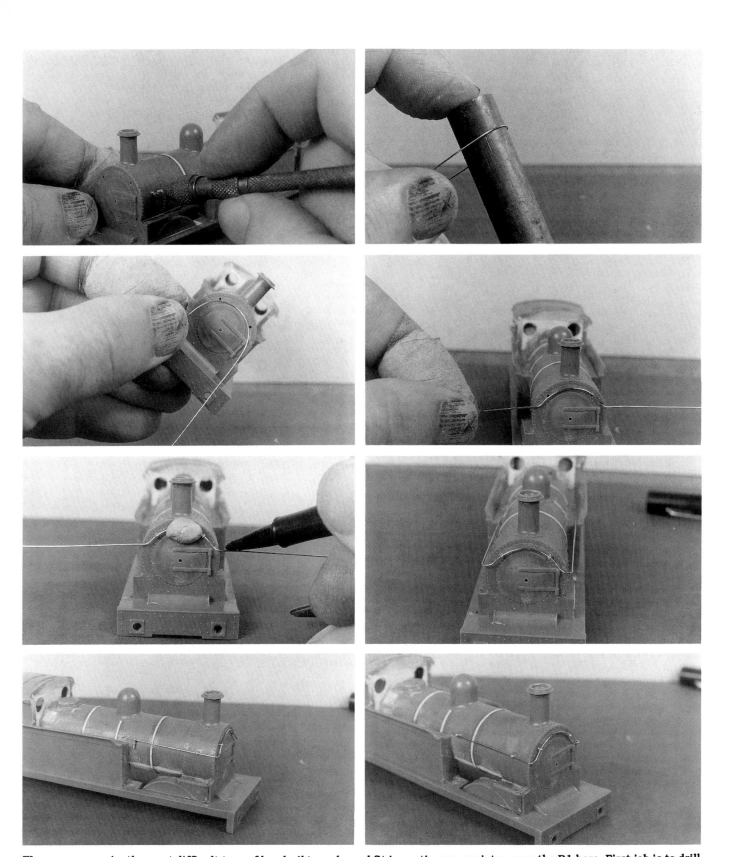

Worse case senario; the most difficult type of handrail to make and fit is continuous variety, as on the R1 here. First job is to drill the necessary holes, as this rail was replacing a carved-off moulded version. The curve of the smoke box portion of the rail is then formed in the middle of a length of suitable wire - this is John Flack's 0.45mm nickel silver - using a piece of dowelling (considerably undersized to allow for 'spring'). After trial fitting to the smokebox, the horizontal bends in the front portion can be made. To determine the position of the critical 'round the corner' bends, the rail is secured to the smokebox with Blue Tak and the locations marked with felt pen or Chinagraph pencil. Before you make the bends, don't forget to thread on the smokebox front handrail knob(s)! The horizontal portions of the rail can then be fitted with stanchions, trimmed to length and finally secured. For this P4 model, I'm using scale size handrail knobs from Alan Gibson.

rails that I fit to RTR locos thus. I do this *after* fitting the rails, brushing on gun blue thinned to a slurry and leaving it to act for a minute or so, then thoroughly washing the residue away under the running tap. Even where the rail will be painted (as most prototype rails were) I blacken them, as the paint will stick to blackened brass much better than to the untreated metal. Gun blue will blacken brass, steel and nickel silver, but not solder or glue. This doesn't matter if you're painting the rails, which I usually am - paint sticks pretty well to solder and dried cyano without any help. If you do find it necessary to blacken solder, then Carrs now do an appropriate potion called, unsurprisingly, 'Solder Black'.

Lamp Irons

I have not yet met the RTR model that comes equipped with a decent set of

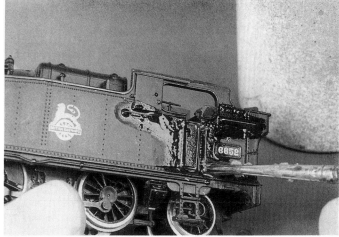

In-situe blackening : Gun Blue is applied carefully with a small brush, allowed to act, then washed off with copious supplies of water.

lamp irons. The fact that some such models come fitted with any sort of lamp irons at all would have caused amazement not so many years ago, but there's no getting away from the fact that these are a fitting that does not lend itself to mass production. So, we tend to get either moulded on 'low relief' lamp irons, or freestanding efforts of decidedly chunky aspect, as on the old Mainline 43XX Mogul. In either case, I lop 'em off, as my standard calls for proper metal strip to replicate a feature that is, at full size, simply that: flat strip.

The material I use is fine brass or nickel silver strip, usually John Flack's 0.87mm wide by 10thou. thick, which is just about right for size. Where the bracket is of the formed variety, with a support tongue on which the lamp sits, then I sometimes opt for a thinner material, as it will be used in double thickness, as shown in the sketch. Wherever possible, I keep the bracket attached to the length of strip from which it has been made until after it is in place on the loco, especially when using the 'melt in' method of attachment. I either make a nick with a triangular needle file across the strip at the point where I wish it to separate from the strip, or, where I can get at it after fixing, I use the Xuron snips to cut off the surplus.

The GWR, of course, were as cussed in the matter of lamp irons as they were about everything else, and so used a system of side mounted lamps rather than the rear mounting arrangement that was good enough for everybody else. These brackets were on the *left* side of the lamps as you looked at them bullseye-on, and so were offset to the offside of the loco at the front, and to the nearside at the rear. I know this, you know this, everybody knows this; and *still* I get it wrong three times in ten! These offset GW brackets are a particular pain at the rear, where bunker back or tender brackets have a flat right angle bend in them. I suppose Swindon made this by some blacksmithery, and I do much the same, using either a soft grade of brass strip, or strip that has been softened

by heating. You can then simply bend it 'in the flat', hammering out any distortion afterwards.

Or, alternatively, you can use thinner strip and adopt the dodge shown in the sketch.

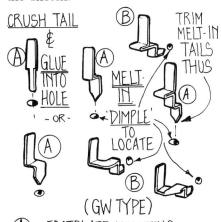

Lamp Irons

Fixing Lamp Irons.

There are two options here; you either drill a hole and glue the things in place with a suitable adhesive, or you can melt them in using the small soldering iron and the set of melt in jigs that are coming up in a paragraph or two. If you opt to glue lamp irons in place, then the best adhesive is a gel cyano or a liquid epoxy. The real problem is that the tail of the bracket, being flat strip, doesn't make a very good fit in your hole, which will anyway need to be drilled to a diameter equivalent to the width of the strip. This makes the hole rather large and obtrusive, and doesn't actually give a very strong fixing. I have found that it's much better to crush the tail of the bracket into a sort of square shape (actually, it's more like a 'U' section channel), which makes a much better fit into a smaller hole. Fine serrated jaw pliers are the best tool for this crushing job, but it yours are smooth jawed, you can crush the strip effectively by using the very

root of the jaws next to the pivot, as in the picture.

Melting in Detail

This I have found to be a very fundamental technique for detailing plastic

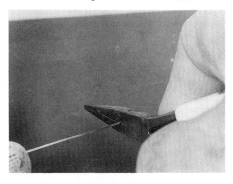

models with metal components, and I use it very widely when reworking RTR locos. The principle is very simple - one simply uses a small soldering iron to heat up the metal component until it

The melt-in technique is ideal for fixing lamp irons. Those of the 56XX, shown here, are located as in the diagram, and gently pushed home with the tip of a small soldering iron, keeping the lamp iron attached to the remainder of the strip from which it is formed to give a 'handle'. Once in place, the excess strip is snipped away with Xuron shears.

Typical melt-in details are the grab-irons on my US F7 A diesel. These are located into start marks or dimples, some of which are provided on this Athearn model. In the first picture, the grab has one 'leg' made longer then the other and this is located and melted in first. Once the fitting is positioned, it is melted home using the Formica jigs for spacing. The same procedure was adopted for the much smaller grabs either side of the unit's nose door. As the last picture shows, this model finished up with a *lot* of melted-in detail.

is hot enough to melt the plastic of the moulding at the point where it is in contact with it. The metal detail is then gently pushed home with the tip of the soldering iron, which is modified with a series of non-slip grooves especially for this purpose, as sketched in the tool section way back in chapter 2. Also sketched in chapter 2 are the selection of little melt in aids or jigs filed up from scraps of Formica, which I find immensely useful both to protect the model from making too close an acquaintance with the tip of the soldering iron, and for locating the component being melted in.

To aid initial positioning of the melt in tails of details like grab irons or lamp brackets, I usually drill a little tiny 'pilot dimple' to give a non-slip location for the component that will keep it in the right spot until the plastic parts like the Red Sea and swallows it up. As can be seen from the picture sequence, I don't start with the jig in place, but grip the component in tweezers or, in the case of lamp irons, by the uncut remainder of the strip from which it's made. There are a couple of other dodges to aid initial location of the detail. On lamp irons, I use the Xuron snips or a file to shape the tail to a point, so that it will engage accurately in my drilled pilot dimple. To locate grab irons, I make one 'leg' longer than the other, so that the component only needs to be 'started' at one end to achieve basic positioning; the second end can then be adjusted independently, rather than trying to get both ends in the right place in one go.

Once the detail is 'started in' to the surface of the model, I select the appropriate Formica jig, and position this

to protect the model and to space the grab, lamp iron or whatever accurately and consistently out from the surface of the model. With a bit of practice, it's surprising how quick, accurate and effective this technique can be. The occasional component might actually finish up a bit loose in its self-melted socket, but a drop of cyano applied with the tip of a pin is almost always enough to effect a cure. The only other remedial action that might be needed is to remove a build up of displaced molten plastic around the entry point of the component. This is usually only a problem where you're melting in either larg(ish) section components, or where the tail goes very deep into the moulding. Either way, the tip of a sharp craft knife or scalpel blade will carve it away. As with the glued or force-fitted handrails, I chemically blacken strip lamp irons or wire grabs with gun blue once they're fixed in place.

Bufferbeam Upgrades

The bufferbeams of RTR locos are typically amongst the most unsatisfactory areas of the model. The universal fitment of the awful tension-lock coupling has a lot to answer for in this direction, especially on diesel locos, which tend to be very busy about the bufferbeam. Substituting a simple wire loop at the appropriate height (8mm above rail level) will not in any way compromise the operational capabilities of the loco, but will enable this area of the model to be properly detailed, which makes a huge difference. The fitment of such loops is covered under the chassis upgrades in a page or two.

The moulded plastic buffers fitted to

many RTR locos are actually pretty good, and substitution by turned items isn't necessarily an improvement, especially where there are details such as ribs or footsteps on the buffer housings. Given that, where tension-lock or Peco-type couplings are in use, the buffers are purely decorative, then metal buffers have no advantage per se. The main cosmetic blights afflicting RTR moulded plastic buffers are a mould part line across the buffer faces, and an unsightly waisted gap where the buffer housing - usually a separate moulding - joins the buffer base moulded onto the beam. I often break these buffers off, file the mating end square, and re-cement, aiming to get a seamless fit. If you run plenty of liquid cement around the joint, it will usually form a nice fillet by dissolving the adjacent plastic. Once dry and painted, the appearance is of buffer housings and bases that are a single unit, as on the prototype.

Only where the buffers fitted to the RTR model are unsatisfactory or just plain wrong do I replace them on cos-

Mould part lines across buffer faces are very obvious, and a little work with scraper and sanding stick to remove them is well worth while.

Badly fitted moulded buffers on RTR locos are best snapped off, filed true, and cemented back in place with Daywat Poly. Using a generous application of solvent allows the joint to fill out with dissolved plastic elliminating gaps.

metic grounds. Occasionally, however, if reworking a loco to use either scale three link couplings, or auto-couplers such as the Jackson, when the buffers assume functional significance, I may decide to modify or replace them. This is usually where the loco in question is destined to shunt on sharply curved track, when I have found that *softly* sprung buffers can help avoid buffer locking. To this end, I opt for the Kean-Maygib or Gibson turned sprung buffers, both of which use a very soft miniature coil spring. Very often, I'll content myself with fitting the turned heads and springs into the moulded plastic buffer housings of the RTR model, suitably drilled out.

Other bufferbeam upgrades usually include the provision of a properly modelled set of vacuum and steam heat connections. All vacuum standards are *not* the same, though you'd never know it from studying most models, where the same old stock mass-produced fitting turns up willy-nilly. The other bufferbeam feature conspicuously absent from most RTR models is the screw or 3-link coupling. It's sobering to realise that vintage Hornby-Dublo tender locos, ostensibly toys, did without front auto-couplers, sporting instead a representative hook and figure '8' link that at least gave the impression of a screw coupling. This feature alone elevated Dublo engines several points up the desirability scale in my youthful eyes! Why contemporary Hornby A4s are disfigured by pointless front tension-locks and totally bereft of any representation of even the coupling hook - so prominent on the prototype - is beyond me. Just ditching the tension-lock and supplying a scale screw coupler makes a huge difference to this model.

Modern diesel locos go several stages further in the bufferbeam complication

stakes, with air, power and multiple unit lines in addition to basic brake hoses. Most modern locos also have buckeye couplers in addition to the screw type, and I'm amazed that more modellers of the contemporary scene don't adopt the American Kadee working buckeye coupler, which looks fine in a modern UK context, functions far better than any old tension-lock, and gives a much closer to scale coupling distance. I also use American HO multiple unit, electrical and airline bufferbeam fittings by Detail Associates; these are moulded in flexible plastic, and are neat, well detailed and easy to fit. They may not be spot-on for a 4mm British diesel, but they look pretty good to my eye.

Making Bufferbeam Detail

Fortunately, most of the characteristic fittings found on locomotive bufferbeams can be fairly easily made. Which is just as well, as these are details which the trade often can't supply in satisfactory form. I can't abide flimsy cast whitemetal vacuum or steam heat connections, and the alternative Oriental turned brass items, while nicely made, are not appropriate in a great many cases. I would maintain that making an accurately modelled set of bufferbeam fittings adds both authenticity and individuality to any RTR model, steam or diesel.

The basic material for making vacuum or steam heat connections is wire, in a variety of grades and sizes. We need something of an appropriate size to form the 'core' of the fitting, plus some fine soft wire with which to model the reinforcing ribs of a vacuum hose, and the joints and connections on both steam and vacuum fittings. As a core for vacuum hoses, I often use straightened-out paper clips; these are made of a softish mild steel or iron wire, which comes in a variety of diameters dependent upon the size of the clip. Cultivate a catholic collection of clips, as I do, and you'll find something appropriate to every occasion.

For the bindings that will represent unions, reinforcing ribs and so on, I use fine copper wire, culled from offcuts of fine electrical flex. Loudspeaker cable (which you can buy by the metre from hi-fi shops) often has a core consisting of very many strands of very fine copper wire. A few inches of 70-strand speaker flex will make you an awful lot of vacuum pipes! An alternative source of fine copper wire - not quite as delicate as the 40 gauge strands from speaker wire, but still acceptably fine - is our old friend five amp fuse wire, a modeller's detailing aid that dates back to the days of John Ahern and the 4mm scale modelling pioneers.

Making Vacuum Standards

The actual method for making a typical vacuum standard is illustrated in the picture sequence. The forming of the core armature to the correct shape is the most critical part of the business, as it's this that forms the most distinctive prototype difference between the standards fitted to full sized engines. The GW low pattern front vacuum standard, for instance, with its hose in a tight arc offset to the dummy receptacle just by the base of the offside front buffer, is very distinctive. Fit a GW loco with the usual commercial straight up and down standard, and it looks most odd. I *always* work from photographs when modelling vacuum or steam heat pipes, as I'm interested in how they appeared in service, not how some draughtsman thought they should look!

As will be apparent from the photo sequence, it's a great help when winding on the reinforcing binding to vacuum hoses to bend this armature core in such a way that it's attached to the rest of the wire from which it's formed at the coupling end. This enables you to wind on the copper wire binding on a straight, unobstructed section of wire, rather than trying to fiddle it round the curved portion of the vacuum connection. You don't need to make the windings tight or particularly accurate, as they can simply be pushed up to the required final position rather like granny's knitting on her ever-clicking needle.

However, if possible, it is best to wind the entire vacuum hose binding from a single length of fine copper wire, as disguising joints in mid-hose is not at all easy. Once the binding of copper wire is complete, it is secured in place by soldering it to the core wire. I brush on a liberal dose of phosphoric acid flux, load the iron with a small blob of solder and touch it to the ends of the binding. The solder will nip along the length of the hose, securing the binding along it's length. Make sure that you don't flood the copper binding with too much solder; if needed, you can always add a spot more, but trying to remove excess which may mask detail is none too easy.

Pipe unions or flanges can now be added by winding on a few turns of the fine copper wire, and fixing these in place with a reasonably generous blob of solder which will take away the 'wound wire' look that's inappropriate for these fittings. That only leaves securing brackets, formed in fine brass strip (the stuff used for lamp irons does nicely) as in the sketch. Make sure that you get the 'waist' of the bracket behind the upright as tight as possible, otherwise the bracket will push the standard too far off of the bufferbeam. If you need a really secure mounting for this standard, you may want to modify this bracket as described in the 'securing' paragraph.

Steam Heat Fittings

Steam heat pipes are made and de-

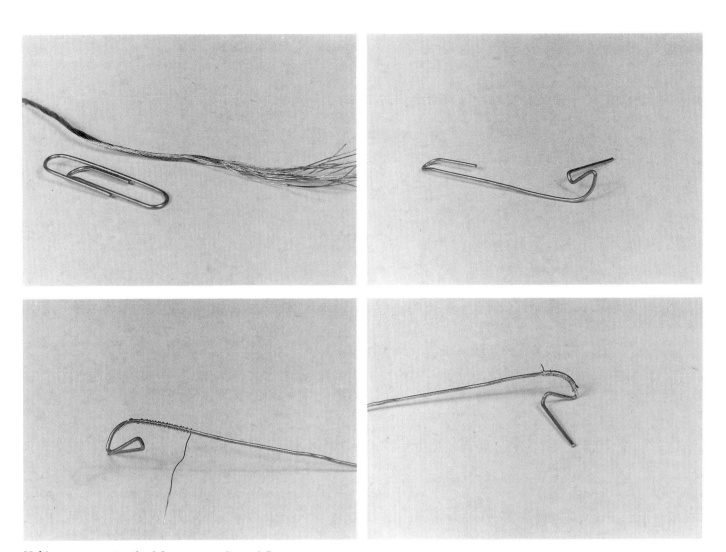

Making vaccum standard from paper clip and flex.

tailed in much the same way, except that, in a lot of cases, they aren't bound with wire in the same way as a vacuum hose. This is because, in contrast to a *vacuum* hose, which has to be reinforced against collapsing inwards, steam hoses have to resist internal pressure, which is often achieved by a wrapping of flat reinforcing bandage rather than by the provision of those prominent wire ribs. Look at your prototype pictures to see what type of hose your particular engine uses. The GWR actually helps modellers in this instance, as they tended to remove steam heat connections in the summer months, so model your layout in July and save yourself some work! All that shows in this instance is the end of the train steam heat pipe and a flange - I've modelled it thus on my panniers.

Bufferbeam vacuum and steam heat pipes don't exist in isolation - there will be accompanying pipework on the rest of the loco, often running along the footplate angles. Steam heat pipes were often lagged - a nice little modelling challenge described in the 'pipework' notes in just a moment. Be aware when forming the armatures for your bufferbeam hoses of the need to leave a long enough 'tail' to connect up with this pipework - such connections are often very visible. At all events, you need a long enough tail to secure the whole fitting to the model, so if in

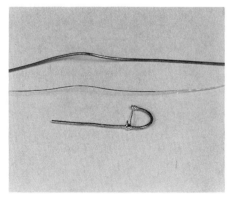

The ingredients of a steam heat hose are basically as for a vaccum pipe, except that thinner core wire will often be needed.

doubt, leave yourself plenty of leeway and clip off the excess later.

Securing Bufferbeam Fittings

These are often horribly vulnerable, especially if you're using 3-link couplings, and need to be very firmly fixed in place. Obviously, as these fittings vary a good deal in size, form and location, it's difficult to suggest a universal method. However, what is set in a tablet of stone is that only when the whole fitting is complete and ready to be secured in place on the model do I cut off the surplus core wire from either end of the armature. The Xuron snips are the ideal tool for this job, as

they give a nice square end.

Generally, bufferbeam fittings not suitable melt in candidates, and I usually find that a combination of the fuse wire fixing loop (described under 'pipework' in just a moment) and a good blob of epoxy on the tail end of the fitting will do the trick. A drop of cyano where the prototype bracket meets the bufferbeam doesn't go amiss, either. If, however, you are faced with a tall, exposed or otherwise particularly vulnerable vacuum standard, then you may need to provide a beefier fixing. I achieve this by replacing the usual prototype bufferbeam fixing bracket with a split-pin arrangement as in the vacuum pipe fixing sketch, ignoring the part of the bracket that should be rivetted flat to the bufferbeam; if this omission really notices, you can represent this portion of the bracket with a couple of tiny pieces of fine Microstrip welded to the plastic bufferbeam. With the split-pin arrangement firmly soldered to the standard, a suitable hole can be drilled through the bufferbeam, and the whole standard secured with liquid epoxy run into the hole, reinforced with a good blob behind the beam, chassis clearance permitting.

Changing Buffers

If you do find that you need to replace

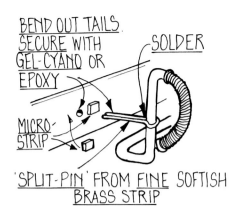

BEND OUT TAILS.
SECURE WITH
GEL-CYANO OR
EPOXY
SOLDER
MICRO-STRIP
'SPLIT-PIN' FROM FINE SOFTISH BRASS STRIP

Fixing Vaccum Pipes

the buffers of an RTR model. then this will obviously involve pulling out any turned components and carving off any moulded on buffer housings. This last isn't the easiest of jobs - at least, not on rivetted bufferbeams it isn't. I saw off as much of the offending buffer as possible with the razor or piercing saw, then go over to either a craft knife or, more likely, my sharpened screwdriver, to pare away the remnants of the buffer base moulding. The trick of sticking masking tape over adjoining rivet detail can often help to avoid damage here.

With the RTR buffers out of the way, the next requisite is to drill the beam to take the shanks of the replacements. Don't rely on the RTR makers for correct buffer centres, especially on the older models. This is particularly true of buffer *heights;* Lima, for instance, have an inexplicable and exceedingly aggravating habit of making all their 4mm models sit too high off of the rails - one of the reasons that so many of their models get a thumbs-down from yours truly. On the D8000 (BR TOPS Class 20) diesel that figures below I lowered the ride height of the model to the correct scale distance above the rail - which then put the buffers, compromised for Lima's daft dimensions, too low. So I had not only to cut them off, but to reposition them, as can be seen in the photographs.

When contemplating fitting sprung

buffers to an RTR loco, look out for the need for clearance behind the bufferbeam - which may well not be there. It's not always possible to fit working sprung buffers to RTR models retaining their original chassis but, as I've already pointed out, unless you're using 3-link or Jackson couplings on sharp curves, such buffers are rarely *needed.* I quite often end up locking turned sprung buffers solid with solder and cyano and trimming away the part of the turning which lies behind the beam for fitting to an RTR loco in a purely cosmetic role.

To actually secure new metal buffers to a plastic RTR body, I usually opt for either liquid epoxy or gel cyano, unless the shanks are a very good fit in their holes, when ordinary liquid cyano will do. If you *are* fitting working sprung buffers, fix the buffer housings in place before assembling the buffers; if you don't, it's all China to a glass orange that a bit of glue will get into the buffer and gum up the works. I rarely melt buffers into place, the only exception to this being where the turned base of the buffer housing is too thick. Melting this half into the plastic beam can reduce the visible thickness considerably, although watch out for the displaced plastic forming an unsightly and hard to remove lip around the edge of the base.

Screw Couplings

If a real loco has a screw coupling, especially a highly visible front screw coupling, as on most express passenger classes, then I like to fit one to my model. Unless you regularly go in for double heading or tender first running, then I can't really see the need for obtrusive auto-couplers on the very visible fore ends of such engines. Even then, as already expounded, I'd restrict any such provision to the simple wire loop, and fit the screw coupling cosmetically. I tend to fit only a loop to the rear of tenders, but also provide a hook on the bufferbeam so that the fore end screw couplings can be used functionally for double heading.

On my full house finescale RTR conversions, I use the fiddly but realistic Exactoscale screw coupling (non-work-

ing version!) that is the standard for all my P4 models. On OO models, this type of coupler just doesn't fit in, so I go for something rather more robust, usually either a ready to use Romford, Smiths or Jackson version, or the DIY type from Branchlines. In either case, I usually melt these items into place, tapering the shank to a point and locating it in a drilled dimple as for lamp irons already described.

Many of the better modern RTR locos, such as all the ex-Mainline models and recent introductions in the same vein by Replica and Bachmann, come provided with quite a present-

Screw couplings come in all shapes and sizes. These Smith's versions are a compromise which marry an overscale hook with a rather finer coupling.

able scale coupling hook on their bufferbeams, which I leave in place if I'm fitting the auto-coupler loops. These hooks will actually function with the more delicate 3-link coupler loops if required, but even if destined to remain purely decorative, they do serve to take away that dreadful 'blank' look that used to characterise so many RTR bufferbeams, like a face without a nose. Any such beam I encounter gets at *least* a dummy hook, if not the whole coupling. Every time I see a Hornby A4 my fingers itch!

Pipework

Moulded-on pipework on model locos is rarely satisfying, and I almost always

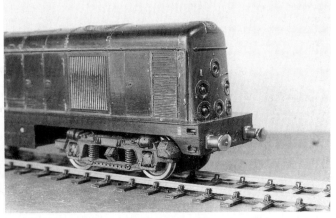

With the Lima Class 20 adjusted to the correct ride height the original buffer locations finish up too low. New buffers are fitted slightly higher on the beam.

The front end of the 56XX, showing the re-detailed buffer beam with new buffers, hoses and screw couplings. The AWS shoe is also in position, as are the lamp irons, sand box linkages, front step grab rails, and the steps on the tank fronts, together with their boiler top grab rails. Much of this detail was melted into place.

opt to carve it off and replace it with fabricated detail in wire. I actually enjoy plumbing locomotives thus, as there's no doubt that properly modelled pipework gives a model a real 'lift', and takes away the mass-produced look. Individually modelled pipe runs will also be just that - individual, an individuality which is a primary aim of all my RTR conversions. The pipe runs on real locos aren't always as neat and tidy as the makers of models would have us believe, and handmade model pipework that incorporates just such slight imperfections will be, well, just that bit more believable.

To make my own pipework, I use wire in all manner of metals and thicknesses, with fine copper wire to make unions and elbows just as for the vacuum standards. I've sketched the most common pipework details, and the methods by which I reproduce them. If you really want to go to town, you can get, from the stockists of US lost-wax brass detail fittings, the most beautiful pipe fittings - unions, elbows and T-pieces. They're a right fiddle to use, but look a million dollars. They cost quite a few dollars, too, and I sometimes feel that going to these lengths on an RTR loco may well come under the heading of a touch too much gilt on the lily. My homemade pipework looks OK, and can be easily tailored to reproduce most prototype pipes, even

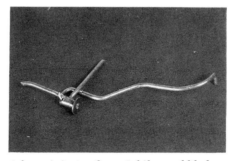

A large injector for a Jubilee, cobbled up from wire as in the sketch.

lagged steam lines. These are quite simply made by wrapping glued strips of fine tissue around a wire core in spiral fashion.

Fixing Pipework

Making nice wire pipework is one thing, but fixing it to moulded plastic RTR bodies is altogether another. My usual method is the fine wire loop, made by wrapping a length of the copper filament wire

around the 'pipe', then twisting the tails together and fixing the lot in place with a sparing application of solder. The solid 'tail' thus produced can be entered into a tiny hole (I use my 0.5mm baseline drill size) and secured with cyano or liquid epoxy, used very parsimoniously. For added security, bend the end of the tail over on the inside of the model, and add a drop more epoxy. The main difficulty with this approach is the difficulty of getting the fixing holes in exactly the right place to line up with the fixing loops; I find that installing these first, then offering the pipework plus fixings up to the model and marking the hole locations with the tip of a sharp scriber is the only reliable method.

Adding Other Metal Details

Various manufacturers, including

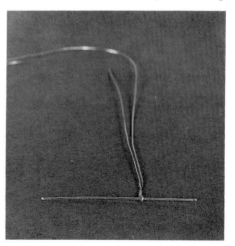

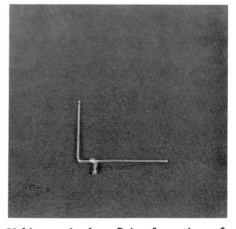

Making a wire loop fixing for a piece of pipework is best done before the pipe is formed to shape. Fine copper wire is wrapped around the pipe, the tails twisted together and soldered, and the excess snipped off. The pipe is then bent to shape.

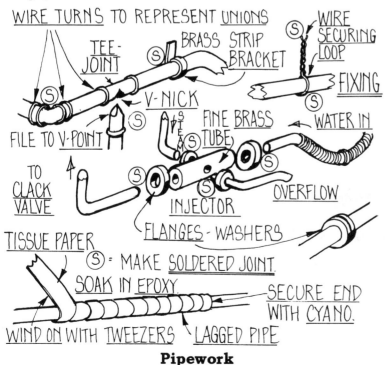

WIRE TURNS TO REPRESENT UNIONS

TEE-JOINT

BRASS STRIP BRACKET

WIRE SECURING LOOP

FIXING

V-NICK

FILE TO V-POINT

FINE BRASS TUBE

WATER IN

TO CLACK VALVE

INJECTOR

OVERFLOW

FLANGES - WASHERS

TISSUE PAPER

(S) = MAKE SOLDERED JOINT.

SOAK IN EPOXY

SECURE END WITH CYANO.

WIND ON WITH TWEEZERS   LAGGED PIPE

Pipework

yours truly under his 'Riceworks' label, have at various times offered a variety of metal detail fittings intended to enhance or convert RTR locos. The main players in this field are Crownline, who offer some quite ambitious conversion kits to enable you to perform quite complex metamorphoses, such as turning your Hornby 9F into a Crosti version. There are a huge selection of such conversions, add-ons, detailing packs and substitutions currently available for both steam and diesel locos, making use of a mixture of plastic mouldings, whitemetal and lost-wax castings and etched components.

Fixing variegated metal fitments firmly to a plastic body calls for a variety of gluing techniques. It's my experience that the chief drawback of a lot of these detail parts is that they don't incorporate positive enough locating and fixing devices, and are thus apt to be a bit fragile when installed. I like to see a good solid peg or pin which can be firmly glued into an appropriate hole drilled in the body moulding. If the casting or whatever lacks such a locating aid, I'll provide it myself by drilling the detail fitting as well as the loco body to take a piece of wire as a reinforcement for what might otherwise be a rather weak joint.

Fixing very small detail, especially castings and tiny etchings such as numberplates or diesel grille covers, can be eased by using an 'instant stick' technique based on UHU and Mek-Pak. If the joining face of such a component is coated with a thin layer of UHU which is allowed to go off, this will enable the part to be stuck to a moulded body using Mek-Pak, treating the part as if it were itself made of plastic. The Mek is introduced on a small brush, and run into the joint by capillary action just as on styrene fabrication work. The Mek dissolves the UHU and makes a welded bond with the plastic surface of the model.

Otherwise, fixing metal details is usually a case of using epoxy or cyano. The thick 'filled' epoxy such as Araldite Rapid is particularly useful in these applications, as it is stiff enough and sticky enough to hold small parts in place while the adhesive cures. Liquid epoxies like 'Strongbond' are apt to let things slide gracefully across the surface of the model unless there is a positive locating aid. All epoxies and the gel cyanos will fill any slight gaps between the detail fitting and the model; ordinary liquid Cyano won't do this, and I only use it for attaching parts that are a really good fit - and those are rare.

Installing Replacement Boiler Fittings

Really, these are just another metal detail, and are attached in much the same way as smaller twiddly bits. With luck, you'll have a nice chunky spigot to work with, which gives you a good leg-up on the locating front. The essential, however, is to get a really good fit between the skirts of chimneys, domes and safety valves, and the top of the smokebox, boiler or firebox. This fit is usually a strong point of RTR locos, and a weak point in many handbuilt models, so it warrants a lot of care and attention to make sure that your 'improvement' doesn't look worse than the original.

The first step is a trial fit to check that the skirt of the fitting sits down properly. If it doesn't, then check first of all that it's the right fitting; it might be something similar designed for a different diameter of boiler. If the error is small, try rolling the skirt of the fitting with the tapered end of a scriber, as in the picture. This is highly effective on whitemetal fittings and also on cast brass where the skirt is reasonably thin. Press down firmly, support-ing the body moulding with a piece of wood wedged in the boiler or smokebox.

You may not be able to get a 100% fit even after this remedial treatment. So long as any misfit is small, then a good result can be obtained by attaching the fitting with thick epoxy, which will fill any small gaps. Eliminating gaps is the main requirement for satisfactory appearance, although ending up with a pronounced 'edge' to part of the skirt of the fitting doesn't help. A bit of dressing-down of the skirt with a round or half round needle file after the epoxy has cured should help to reduce or eliminate any shortcomings of this sort.

Plastikard Detailing

Not all the details we add to our RTR loco bodies will be commercial etched

Using a scriber to roll down the skirt of the replacement Malcolm Mitchell cast white metal chimney fitted to the 43XX.

Another 43XX body, destined for a full P4 conversion, has acquired a Mitchell white metal chimney and safety valve seated down as described and secured with Araldite.

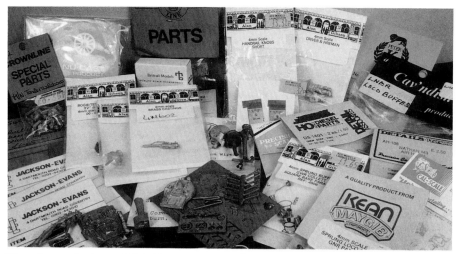

There is no shortage of detailing parts available from the UK and US trade.

Plastikard cube riveting is an effective technique for adding to, or replacing, rivet detail. Here, the cab roof of the 56XX, which has had its original rain strips and rivets carved away, is re-detailed with Microstrip and cube rivets. Once painted, the new detail blends in with the original mouldings.

or cast components. There's quite a lot that we can contrive ourselves with plastic sheet, strip and rod. Toolboxes, AWS battery boxes, extra or replacement steps, cab doors, ventilators or cabside panels and such vital additions as the oft-mentioned fall plate can all be fashioned thus. Really, there's not too much to be said about this type of work, other than that it follows normal Plastikard modelling techniques.

Of these, the most useful are scribing and texturing of sheet plastic to represent wooden floors or other timber components, and the 'minute 10thou. cube' method of adding or replacing rivets. To use this useful technique, you need a really sharp knife, some 10thou. Plastikard sheet (or, better still

vent and the tip of the brush - these embryo rivets are flooded with solvent to 'set' them and round off the edges.

I've sketched some typical Plastikard details as applied to my RTR models, while there are examples of this sort of work dotted hither and thither among the examples. It's surprising just what can be modelled effectively in Plastikard - I've put new pilots, extra hatches, drop steps and all manner of other fittings on my US diesels, and MU fittings, snowploughs, lift brackets and electrical boxes onto British ones. Don't forget that, if need be, Plastikard can be laminated for thickness, and then carved and sanded to shape.

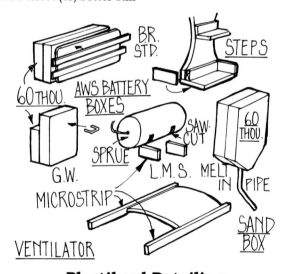

Plastikard Detailing

if you can get it, some 10thou. square Microstrip), a bottle of Mek and a fine (no bigger than No.1) paintbrush. If starting with 10thou. sheet, use your knife and a steel straightedge to cut the finest sliver of a strip you can manage off the edge of the sheet. This whisker of plastic - or the 10thou. square Microstrip - is then chopped finely to give tiny cubes of plastic. These are picked up with the tip of the fine brush, moistened with a quick dip in the Mek, and positioned on the model. Once in place - they can be chivvied about a bit with extra sol-

Cab Interior Detail

A lot of RTR models don't give you much scope in this direction, as the space normally allocated to the crew is full of gurt great whirring motor, especially on tank locos. If this is the case, then the best you can do is to fit in such detail as there's room for. I always try and include at least some representation of the major cab fittings, even if it's only the top third of the backhead plonked on top of the motor as on my 56XX. As just described, I make most of my cab details out of Plastikard, although there are some nice one piece cast boiler backheads that can be cut down if needed.

Otherwise, it's a case of trying to disguise the unprototypical intrusions by positioning crew figures, weather tarpaulins and other distractions between the viewer and the motor. Fortunately, most modern RTR tender locos have unobstructed footplates and, in many cases, quite superbly modelled cab fittings. These can be made a lot more of by careful painting, by adding a crew and such other small but telling details as the RTR makers omit. Don't forget to close up the tender gap and fit a fall plate, as already prescribed.

Fall plates, while not strictly a cab interior detail, are very much part of the rear of *any* tender engine, and for reasons already discussed I consider them a quite vital item of locomotive anatomy. Apart from the simple tongue of Plastikard already described, there are a number of ways in which they can be modelled. I often make them part of a 'cab interior module' that includes the cab floor, crew, fittings such as reversers, seats and brake stands, plus anything else I get carried away enough to include. On tank locos with removable roofs, such as Mainline's J72 and 57XX, it's delightfully easy to make a fully detailed cab interior as a drop-in module, as I've done with the worked-over Replica pannier produced for **Modelling Railways Illustrated's** Broadwell Green' fine scale OO project layout.

The Crew

A vital fitment on *any* model locomotive, and a traditional modeller's blind spot, is the provision of a crew. If I had a currency note of reasonable denomi-

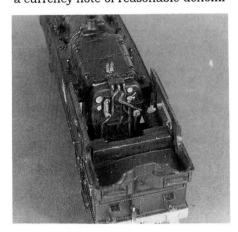

56XX cab interior - cast backhead, Plastikard floor, crew in repose.

nation for every 'ghost train' I've seen on a model railway, I too could afford to buy some nice Japanese brass engines and leave all this plastic hacking behind. However, in the regrettable absence of such easy money, I'll address the problem of employing suitable figures to make good this omission.

After the tension-lock coupling, my number two railway modelling bete noir is that age-old chestnut, the fireman frozen in mid-swing with a shovelful of coal (probably rigid with fright, poor fellow, when he beholds the gaping chasm between loco and tender

aarrrghh...!

into which he is in grave danger of falling...). Nothing, but nothing, looks less convincing than this; I'd rather have a troupe of can-can girls gracing my footplate. But what does virtually every manufacturer of model figures give us for a fireman? Yes, that's right, some poor soul doing the pas-de-deux with the shovel. I despair! But not quite - a large bouquet to Alan Gibson, who supplies a truly excellent set of loco crew figures *in repose,* praise be. I use these Gibson figures as often as I can, but in the interests of variety one must look elsewhere. So I cull likely-looking individuals from all manner of sources and figure ranges (of which the best is undoubtedly Phoenix), and paint and modify them to do duty on the footplates of my models. No loco is allowed out without full ASLEF complement; one or two even rate a shunter or bowler-hatted inspector in addition.

Glazing

Proper glazing of cab windows on both steam and diesel locos is another relatively simple upgrade that has an immense impact on the look of a model. On my American layout, I have a pretty well standard Athearn SW7 switcher, which I have carefully fitted with flush glazing cut from a Fererro Rocher chocolate box. Several people have assumed that it has been upgraded with an expensive aftermarket 'thinwall' cab kit, so dramatic is the effect of the glazing (together with some finer handrails) on the authenticity of the model. This is in spite of the fact that the Athearn model comes as standard with moulded 'flush' glazing, which, as on many RTR models, is really only 'semi-flush'.

There is always a problem trying to mould flush glazing for plastic-bodied models, through the need to incorporate a slight 'taper draft' on the edge of mouldings to aid their release from the moulding tool. The effect of the draft

on the edge of the cab window opening and that on the glazing insert is to give a slight - but highly visible - gap all around the edge of the glazing, as in the sketch. The same is also true of vacuum-formed flush-glazing, such as South Eastern Finecast's 'Flushglaze' - you just don't get an accurate fit between the glazing and the frame which, for me at least, spoils the whole look of a model. So I prefer to file the edges of the window openings square, and cut and file my own glazing inserts from the chocolate box material.

Many better or more recent RTR models do come with good moulded flush glazing, and if this looks well than I leave well alone. Among the best examples in my collection of diesels are the old Mainline 'Warship', which isn't currently available, and the Lima Brush type 2. Glazing on steam locos is less of a problem, as it's less prominent than it is on diesels, but careful flush glazing is still worth fitting. Among RTR makers, Hornby do the best job on their long-running LMS 'Jinty', using the simple expedient of moulding the whole cab in clear plastic and painting the non-window bits of it. Some of my US diesels also use this approach which, moreover, works well on carriages and has much to commend it.

Making and Fitting Flush Glazing

Fitting your own chocolate box flush glazing isn't difficult, just tedious. It all comes down to trial and error, and careful filing and fitting. My usual procedure is to start by filing any taper draft off the edges of the window opening in the moulding, using an appropriately shaped needle file. I then make a crude template by taking a 'rubbing' of the window opening, using an HB pencil and a piece of typing paper. A small scrap of the clear plastic can then be cut, big enough to make the window plus a reasonable margin all round. This chocolate box plastic is fragile, and is best cut with the razor saw used at a shallow angle. Once I've got a suitable blank, I file the window roughly to size, using my 'brass rubbing' template as a guide. Once I get

Before fitting glazing, it is sometimes necessary to reduce the size of a window opening, as on the screens of the Athearn F7A. This reduction is accomplished with square Microstrip, cemented in place with Daywat Poly and reinforced on the inside with Araldite. The strip is set slightly proud and sanded down once in place.

The glazing of the F7A was completed after the model had been painted. Individual glazing units cut from Ferrero Rocher chocolate box are carefully filed to a tight fit, and secured with a drop of Cyano applied with the tip of a pin. The finishing touch is added by the windscreen wipers, made from wire and fixed with Cyano.

pictures in chapter 7 show, you can do a lot with a few scraps of Plastikard, a bit of tissue paper, some thread or fine wire, and a keenly observant eye.

Things like the fireman's bicycle thrown up on the tender of a branch goods engine, the odd bit of timber packing on a rear tender deck, or a shunter's pole looped through the handrails of a shunting engine all add credibility to our models as portraits of the everyday workhorses that they really were. They add the human touch that makes the railway come alive every bit as much as the addition of the all-important crew figures.

Exit the Body Beautiful....

I could go on dissecting the possibilities for embellishing the moulded plastic bodies of our RTR locos with ever more detail, but I think that you'll have

Acrylic glazing, a window in a tin. It is ideal for dealing with small and awkwardly shaped areas of glazing. I tried out my tin on a scrap R1 body - it's quite tricky to use, so practising on something that doesn't matter is a good idea.

close to the finished dimensions, I abandon the template and resort to continual checking against the actual opening.

Make sure that you use the file 'square' when bringing the window down to final size, so that you get a nice tight fit in the opening.

Assuming you've got a good fit, then this plastic glazing can be simply secured with the usual liquid styrene cement, taking care, as always, to apply it sparingly and keep it off the glazed areas. If the fit is a bit so-so, with the odd narrow gap between glazing and frame, then I abandon plastic cement in favour of gap-filling gel cyano (the Americans have a wonderful one called, picturesquely, 'Zap-a-Gap', which you can sometimes find at model aircraft shops. Victors also sell one, sold under a title that is ponderous rather than picturesque: Hot Stuff Super T Gap-filling Cyano-Acrylate Adhesive).

This, if carefully applied with a piece of wire or the tip of a cocktail stick, will run round the edge of the glazing and eliminate the gaps.

Acrylic Glazing

There is a further glazing alternative which is particularly useful for small and awkward windows. This is a clear acrylic compound designed to skin over smallish openings; you run it

round the edge in a thick bead, then draw it across the centre of the opening with the tip of the indispensable cocktail stick. It has a very high surface tension which enables it to form a stable skin across the opening, which can then be left to air dry to form perfectly fitted glazing. It does tend to come out slightly concave on anything much bigger than a typical steam loco porthole cab spectacle, but on those awkward efforts that follow the outline of the boiler it's magic. The one I use is another American product from the friendly folks at Victors, sold under yet another succinct and snappy title as 'Krystal Kleer'. Carr's do a UK equivalent, known, with equal logic, as 'Windowfilm'.

Miscellaneous Finishing Touches

Apart from chassis details and those little embellishments, such as shedplates, lamps or fire irons, that are best considered as part of the painting process, this category covers the little touches that can 'make' a model as a believable portrait of a real engine. Such refinements as modifying cab roof ventilators or cab doors to be open or half-open, providing tarpaulin weathersheets or cabside sliding shutters, toolboxes and other such miscellaneous but necessary fittings are all well worthwhile, and not difficult to execute. As the sketches and

got the drift by now; some good prototype pictures, a well-filled scrapbox and a keen eye are the keys. However, it's no good producing a belter of a body if it has to sit on a chassis that looks awful and runs worse, so to keep things in balance, it's time to take a look at the mechanical bits.

Chapter Six

Chassis Cosmetics

The Bachmann 93XX mogul exhibits most of the strengths and weaknesses of modern RTR locos. A decent wheel profile, balance weights, reasonabley fine rods, a good cross-head and brake gear are the plus points. On the debit side, the cylinders are woefully undersized and the leading truck is unrealistic, with very deep flanges to its wheels. The results of the modifications to this loco can be seen in the picture of the finished model which headed chapter 4.

Obviously, before worrying too much about what the chassis looks like, it's necessary to make sure it runs as well as possible. The whole business of getting the best mechanical performance from the current and not so current generation of RTR locomotive chassis is wide ranging, covering motor parameters, pick-up, gearing and wheels. This proved to be a rather more complex and far-reaching area than could be properly covered within a book essentially concerned with the cosmetics of RTR models.

I did try it, mind - but soon realised, as the first draft of the intended chapter roared past the 10,000 word mark with no end in sight, that the whole business of RTR loco mechanics merited a separate book. So a companion volume to this one is now in prospect, covering the overhaul, tuning-up, rectification, improvement, rewheeling and even total replacement of RTR loco chassis. Which means, for the moment, that attention is focused on those aspects of the RTR chassis which are less the wonderful to *look* at.

Undersized Cylinders

These aren't an occasional ailment among RTR models, they're a full-blown epidemic. Of the outside cylindered models in my collection (Mainline 43XX and Bachmann 93XX GW Moguls, two Replica B1s, Mainline Jubilee, Hornby B17 and Shire), not

one came from the makers with correctly proportioned cylinders. Some, such as the 93XX above, have cylinders that are so undersized they're a joke; were there a real piston on the end of that piston rod, it'd burst through the front cover the first time the wheels turned! Here, then, is yet another of those little mysteries surrounding the design of many of our RTR locos; on none of the models listed can I see any logical or pressing reason for fitting these undernourished lungs, except perhaps on the B17, where they're sacrificed for trainset-style bogie swing.

Even here, though, it's the overscale flanges on the scale diameter bogie wheels that cause the real problem, not the size of the cylinders. When are our RTR (and kit, if it comes to it) designers going to wake up to the basic and elementary fact that it is the *overall* wheel diameter (tread diameter plus flange) that counts on the clearance front? Hornby-Dublo cottoned on to that one way back in 1938, one reason why scaled-up Dublo locos always look right. By fitting undersize (on the tread) wheels, Dublo designers were able to keep the essential clearances, cylinders, splasher sizes and so on of their locos correct to scale - for which design nous generations of modellers may be thankful. So my 'Duchess of Atholl' (vintage 1948) will charge happily around 15 inch radius curves, yet has cylinders that are within 0.5mm

of dead scale on all dimensions. Also (sorry to harp on about it, but there it is...) the cylinders of my twenty five pound Mehanotechnica USRA Pacific are also the correct scale size. These are bigger than on *any* UK loco, and physically bigger in 3.5mm/ft than any 4mm cylinder I've yet met, yet the model will still run on 18 inch radius curves. There's a moral there somewhere!

Correcting Undersized Cylinders

The cylinders on the otherwise excellent Mainline Jubilee that forms the main example here are anything but scale size on any dimension; they're 1mm below scale top to bottom and 2mm short over the end covers (nearer 3mm short over the valve chests). This sort of error - at its worst, the thick end of a foot at full size - can completely spoil the whole look and proportional balance of an engine, and the difference brought about by fitting cylinders of the correct size verges on the dramatic. By and large, once you've added the necessary missing inches, which nowadays is a simple matter, your problems are more or less over. A change of bogie wheels or a little flange reduction may be needed, but slidebars, crossheads, rods and valve gear aren't affected.

This happy state of affairs comes about thanks to another of our resourceful independent hobby traders.

Comet models produce a whole range of locomotive components, including, if required, complete chassis kits. Using the cylinders from these, which are available separately, correcting undersized cylinders is no problem. The all-metal Comet cylinders are simply adapted to form scale size overlays for the undernourished plastic cylinders of the RTR locos.

Comet's cylinders have etched brass ends with nicely detailed cast whitemetal wrappers, valve chests and valve spindle brackets (where these are appropriate). In the case of the Jubilee, their standard LMS-pattern cylinders were absolutely spot-on.

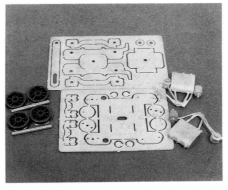

A new set of cylinders and front bogie for the Jubilee, courtesey of Comet Models and Kean Maygib, whose wheels these are.

As can be seen from the photo-sequence, the work required to adapt these Comet cylinders to their new role is really quite straightforward. The basic idea is to retain the basic RTR moulded plastic cylinder, suitably filed down, as a 'core' for the metal overlay. This includes the preservation of the moulded cylinder rear, valve chest rear, slidebars and valve spindle bracket. In other words, all the bits that tie up with the Mainline valve gear are left alone, and no functional aspect of the chassis is touched.

I prepare the new overlay first, simply a matter of cutting the Comet stretcher/cylinder end etching to sepa-

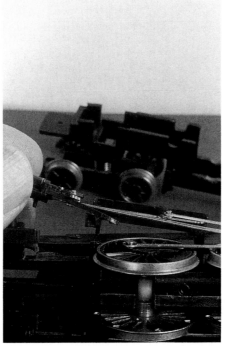

Bringing the Jubilee's cylinders up to size from their stunted starting point is not *really* that difficult. The plastic cylinders are merely pegged to the chassis, and can be removed by carefully disengaging the motion bracket, also pegged to the frame, and sliding the cylinders free of the crosshead. The Comet cylinders are assembled as described in the text, ready for use as overlays to the plastic originals. This calls for considerable paring down of the plastic cylinders. The overlays can then be tried in place to check the fit below the footplate. Once all is well, the overlays are glued to the remnants of the plastic cylinders, and the new cylinder assembly is reunited with the crossheads and valve gear.

rate the fronts of the cylinders. These are then assembled to the cast wrappers by soldering or gluing with epoxy resin, and the cylinder front cover and valve chest detail added. While I'm at it, I also fit the drain cock detail below the cylinder, using wire and fine strip. That completes the new cylinder, which can be cleaned up and painted before fitting.

The plastic Mainline cylinder is now removed from the model. The front valve chest is cut off with the Stanley knife or razor saw, and the remains are then offered up to the backless Comet cylinder. The idea now is to file enough off the width and depth of the moulded cylinder to allow the Comet assembly to sit down over it, in most cases keeping the back of the Comet wrapper level with the rear of the moulded cylinder.

Before you all reach for your best Biros to write in and point out that this will offset the overlay toward the front rather than making it symmetrical about the existing cylinder centreline, I'll anticipate you by pointing out that in a lot of cases, the rear of the RTR cylinder is actually in the right place; it usually has to be, otherwise the crosshead travel and slidebars wouldn't tie up. The 'lost inches' are thus very often at the fore end of the cylinder only, and the existing cylinder centreline is itself incorrect. See how many RTR cylinders don't *quite* line up with their outside steam pipes.

While this offset is conveniently true of the likes of the GW Moguls, the Jubilee, of course, is the exception that proves the rule; it has slidebars that are a 2mm too long, to allow the cylinder rear to move forward a bit and centre the undersize cylinder correctly. As the implications of moving it back to the right place are rather far-reaching, I compromised a bit by allowing the rear of the Comet wrapper to overhang the moulded cylinder rear slightly. This subterfuge is only apparent on close inspection from a three quarter rear viewpoint. The far more prominent fronts of the cylinders are, of course, totally correct.

Adopting the approach of keeping the original plastic cylinders and slidebars intact also addresses another problem with these split-frame chassis, the need to maintain side to side electrical isolation. This means that you can't employ either the Comet cylinders, or any other cast or etched cylinders, as a pair on the metal stretchers with which they are designed. The same is true for Hornby locos - they may not use split frames, but the wheels are hub insulated, which means that the rods and valve gear are live to the respective rails. Bridge these with an all-metal cylinder assembly, and you've got yourself an A1 red alert dead short.

On locos like Hornby's B17, you *can* make use of complete Comet cylinders if you insulate them side for side. Adapting the existing Hornby plastic cylinder stretcher is one possibility, but

I would choose to use a piece of sixteenth inch sheet PCB, suitably gapped. The middle of the Comet stretcher can be simply cut out and replaced with the PCB, making for a strong all-soldered cylinder assembly. However, for reasons of valve gear authenticity which we'll come on to in a moment, I don't find that the combination of dead accurate cylinders with somewhat compromised valve gear works very well, so I prefer to stick with the Hornby cylinders and modify them with Plastikard.

Modifying Cylinders with Plastikard

Building up existing undersized moulded cylinders using Plastikard is the main alternative to replacement or overlaying. This approach is particularly useful in cases like that of Replica's B1, where the cylinders are the right depth and outline with beautiful authentic detailing, but are (for reasons even more inscrutable than usual), 1mm too short. This isn't actually *too* apparent to the eye, so in this case the error could be left without a great penalty. However, if required, it can be corrected. The answer in this case is to reach for the razor saw and divide each cylinder, like Gaul, into three parts, which can then be re-assembled with a piece of 20thou. Plastikard let in at both ends between the centre part of the cylinder and the reinstated front and rear. These Plastikard fillets should be cut over-

size, and finish-filed to the cylinder outline once the cement has cured. Another typical Plastikard modification was that which I applied to the cylinders of the Hornby B17. The Hornby originals are right for length, but in this instance are slightly too shallow. So I made my cut horizontally beneath the valve chest, and let in a fillet of 50thou. Plastikard between the chest and the main cylinder barrel.

I had to cut a clearance in this fillet to take the Hornby slidebar, and I also filed off the undersized cylinder front cover from the Hornby moulding, replacing it with a disc of 20thou. Plastikard of the correct diameter, which in turn called for a little packing to the rear of the cylinder moulding. This new front cover helped to weld the assembly into a single, strong unit. The horizontal fillet was filed flush with the Hornby casing, and the prominent cleading bolts on these cylinders, which Hornby miss off, were added in Plastikard cubes.In conjunction with this correction, I found I needed to fit new bogie wheels, with smaller flanges (and the correct number of spokes - 12 instead of 10); my new wheels came from Ultrascale.

Improving Rods and Valve Gear

Once the cylinders are sorted out as to size and location, the obvious next step is to look at the associated slidebars, crossheads, connecting and coupling rods, and the valve gear, if any. This is an aspect of miniature locomotive production which has, traditionally, sorted out the models from the toys. Once again, back in the old days, Hornby-Dublo made the grade as models to a far greater extent than their rivals. They *always* gave you a full set of working Walshaerts, even if it was rather chunky. By the standards of the day, these Dublo valve gears were highly regarded, and a lot of reputable scale modellers used to adapt and fit Dublo valve gear to kit or scratchbuilt models. Trix and Triang, on the other hand, only did half a job, with crude and greatly-simplified representations of the wily Belgian's waggling wonder. Most of the waggly bits on these simplified gears didn't waggle, and not surprisingly, they never looked very good.

This is an area in which great strides have been made in recent years. The detailed cast crossheads, well-proportioned coupling and connecting rods and relatively delicate valve gear were one of the aspects of my Mainline Jubilee that so impressed me back in 1982. But even that standard of excellence pales a trifle when compared to the scale size rods and delightfully delicate and detailed Walshaerts on Replica's B1, which I rate as the best valve gear I've yet seen on a mass-produced RTR model. And yes, that does include my much-bandied Mehanotechnica USRA light Pacific!

Hornby Valve Gears

While Hornby's rods and valve gear - as typified by the B17 - don't reach the very high standard set by Mainline and Replica, they are still a very great deal better than their efforts of not so long since. Where they lose out is in being an awful lot chunkier in outline, and by incorporating major compromises of layout. For a start, Hornby still persist with their rather crude design of coupling rod, which has force-fitted crankpins at both ends of the rod running in holes in the wheels. This is the reverse of the prototypical arrangement of the rod running on the pin, as used by Replica et al. If you change the wheels on a Hornby loco, these rods need reworking to take 'proper' crankpins. Sets of decent scale etched 'aftermarket' rods to match the various Hornby chassis would be a useful product, should one of our cottage industrialists feel inspired to come to the aid of the RTR loco modifier...

Hornby's valve gear is still badly compromised in layout and lacking in detail. It is generally arranged in a non-prototypical manner which has the valve rod - which should be able move to and fro - tied in with brackets or other fixed parts of the gear. Admittedly, not even Replica arrange the valve rod so that it *does* move (Dublo did, in 1948), but it at least looks as if it *could*. The Hornby arrangements often look odd because they're usually plain wrong. These gears are also rather too chunky to look realistic - especially in the matter of the rivets holding them together. Many Hornby locos also suffer from the lack of a decent crosshead - there's usually only a simplified pressed metal representation or a crude plastic moulding.

ous ex-Mainline LMS 4-6-0s, for instance, suffer from unwanted heaviness about their valve rods and, particularly, the combination lever (see Walshaerts diagram for an explanation of these terms). This is odd, really, as the rest of the gear, especially the eccentric rod, is very delicate.

The answer to these ills is really very

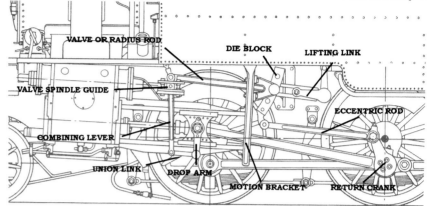

Walschaerts Valve Gear

Slimming Down The Bits

In between Hornby and Replica, representing the two extremes of modern RTR valve gears, come a wide selection of locos fitted with valve gears that, while basically satisfactory, could do - like your author - with shedding a few excess inches here and there. The vari-

simple - just take a file to the various over-heavy bits and whittle 'em down to more satisfactory proportions. Before you all freeze in horror at the thought of attacking something as complex and delicate as a 4mm scale model Walshaerts gear with a file, I'll point out that there's no need to take the thing apart. Indeed, in a good many

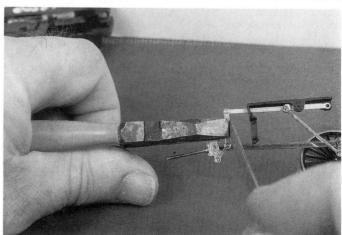

Refining valve gear generally calls for its removal from the loco. The Jubilee comes apart in a fairly typical manner : The keeper plate and cylinders are removed and the wheels, complete with motion, lifted out. It is rarely necessary to separate the valve gear from the wheels and rods, so long as the parts to be filed down can be securely gripped, as in the last picture.

cases, you don't actually *need* to take it off the engine, so long as you disengage it from the cylinders or any holding brackets to a sufficient extent to get at the bits you want to file down. That said, I find it a lot easier to take the valve gear right off, so I usually do. The pictures of the Jubilee getting the treatment should give an idea of what's involved.

With the cruder Hornby valve gears, such as that on the B17, you may need to go a bit further. On this particular engine, the crosshead is merely a bit of bent metal, while the valve rod is combined unrealistically with the pivot bracket for the die block. Apart from any other consideration, this brings the rod far too far out towards the edge of the footplate framing - it should be tucked in some way back. The gear also lacks any representation of the valve spindle bracket and the lifting links behind the die block, a rather prominent feature of these engines.

What I did to reduce the impact of these toy-like compromises can be seen in the pictures. Without undertaking a rebuild so complex that it would be more difficult than fitting a completely new valve gear built up from commercial etchings - probably the best option with most Hornby locos, but somewhat outside the scope of this book - it isn't possible to correct basic errors like the fixed and wrongly located valve rod or the crude crosshead. Some of the missing bits, however, can be added.

In these cases, the best bet is to disguise as far as possible the anomalies. This I did on the B17 by adding a few extra parts in Plastikard, and by painting and weathering the bright metal valve gear parts differentially to disguise their 'all in one' construction.

Paint doesn't stick too well to this bright metal, so I start by brushing on a layer of gun blue to dull the metal and provide a key. The blue does just that on these steel rods, but if you wash and wipe it down, then follow it up with a thin coat of paint in an oily brown, the effect is quite realistic. Painting the die block pivot bracket matt black and leaving the valve rod dull metal draws attention away from the fact that they're all one part. In fact, I find that toning down these Hornby gears with paint and metal black goes a long way to taking away the worst of their toy-like appearance.

The other big let-down on the B17 is the crosshead, which, on the real engine, runs *between* a paired slidebars rather than *outside* a single set as Hornby have it. I disguised this error by building on the missing outer slidebars, using Plastikard Microstrip on 60thou. Plastikard spacer blocks stuck to the Hornby slidebars with cyano. Plastikard is fine for this job, as these extra bars are purely decorative - the original Hornby pressed metal bars take all the mechanical loading.

The missing lifting links behind the die block were also added in Plastikard, built off the bottom of the footplate on the body moulding. A small piece of Microstrip cyano'd to the front of the valve rod at the position of the support bracket - which Hornby acknowledge with a small 'ear' on top of the rod - completes the add-on detailing. Not a lot, but every little helps.

These shortcomings of the running gear on this Hornby loco throw up quite a few problems and possibilities. Really, in the interests of consistency, were this model to be run alongside the likes of the Replica B1, I would prefer to ditch the Hornby rods and

valve gear altogether, along with the cylinders and the bogie, and replace them all with better parts from Comet.

Better Bogies

The bogies and pony trucks fitted to RTR locos are frequently far from accurate representations of the prototype arrangements. The GWR's bar framed bogies and leading trucks, for instance, with their open and airy look, are quite distinctive, and aren't best modelled with slabs of solid plastic. Only the standard-setting Replica B1 among my collection has a bogie with any pretensions to accuracy - at least, it does when you've removed the usual gross tension-lock and mounting pad, a job which thankfully takes mere seconds. The rest, however, including my cherished Jubilee, are decidedly lacking in this respect, and I find a change of

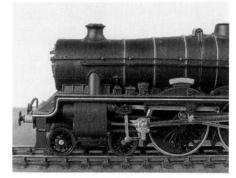

A bogie of prototypical outline, from Comet, improves the authenticity of the Jubilee's front end. The new bogie was fitted using a 6 BA bolt and nut in place of the moulded plastic spindle of the original. The bogie coil spring was shortened to suit the new arrangement. The job was finished with a set of Kean Maygib bogie wheels, the right size and with the right number of spokes.

bogie well worthwhile. Comet, as usual, provide the readiest answer, with nice simple etched bogies and pony trucks for most popular prototypes.

I've already mentioned the business of scale sized bogie wheels with overscale flanges creating clearance problems. They also look wrong, as the eye 'reads' the total diameter of the wheel. Unfortunately a tradition seems to have evolved of late, putting deeper flanges on bogie and leading truck wheels than are fitted to the driving wheels. Another little mystery - will I never divine the reasoning that guides(?) our RTR designers? Even Replica, on the pick-of-the-bunch B1, are guilty of this, while Hornby carry it to extremes; the flanges on the B17's bogie wheels verge on the monstrous.

Needless to say, this is another aspect of the RTR loco chassis requiring cosmetic correction, either by reducing the flanges of the existing wheels, or by binning them in favour of something better. Obviously, if you're rewheeling the driving axles on a loco chassis, then any bogies or trailing trucks (not forgetting also the tender chassis) will need to be equipped with

Modifications to the B17 valve gear depend on fooling the eye. By adding dummy outer slide bars and lifting links in Plastikard, together with overlaying and painting the 'fixed' parts of the motion, the unrealistic 'all in one piece' look of the gear is mitigated.

matching wheelsets. More often, however, the drivers of an RTR loco are acceptable, but the carrying wheels aren't.

What you do about this depends on the other quality aspects of the offending wheelsets. Do they have the right number and shape of spokes? Are they the right size, or just the nearest the manufacturer happened to have in production at the time? Do they run true, or do they wobble about like an expiring Aylesbury in a thunderstorm? And, most importantly, do they look good, or are they a jarring note? Assuming affirmative answers to these questions, then a quick course of flange reduction is all that's needed.

If, however, the factory fitted bogie wheels fail at one or more of these hurdles, then the bin beckons once more, and some replacements must be sought down at the model shop. When choosing replacement wheels, as well as finding something that is the right size and has the right number and shape of spokes, you also need to choose wheels that will 'live happily' with the drivers. This means that you want a tyre profile not too far removed from that of the drivers - ruling out Sharman wheels, which come only to EMf (EM fine, a closer to scale wheel for EM use) or P4 standards. You also want a tyre material of a metal colour that accords with the drivers, which often rules out Ultrascale's nickel silver tyred wheels, which have a decidedly golden tinge to them.

Fitting Replacemen Carrying Wheels

The two ranges of carrying wheels that I find most compatible with standard RTR drivers are Gibson's and Kean-Maygib. These have turned steel tyres on moulded centres, and are made to the standard EM/fine OO profile. The tyres of these wheels often come chemically blackened, but this can be burnished off with fine abrasive paper. Mount the wheel on its axle, and clamp it in a mini-drill or other means of rotating it - the classic 'handbrace clamped in vice' or even a normal DIY power drill will do. The wheel is then rotated at a decently high speed (hard work on the handbrace, I'm afraid!) and wet and dry paper of about 320 grit is used to gently polish off the blackening from the tread. Leave it in place on the front and rear of the tyre, though, as it will help paint to stick.

Gibson and Kean-Maygib carrying wheels use a 2mm axle diameter, which is some way below the 3mm plastic used on Mainline, Bachmann and Replica bogies, but identical to Hornby's steel items. If you need to fit 2mm axles to a Mainline-type bogie, Sharman wheels do a 2mm bore, three thirty second inch outside diameter bearing that can be used to take up the slack. Similar bearings can also be obtained from Perseverance. The Comet bogies and trucks that I use in

place of the moulded plastic originals will take a 2mm axle as they come.

Tender wheels on Mainline, Bachmann and Replica locos also seem frequently to come into the 'chunky flange' category. Usually, assuming that they're otherwise OK for size, spoke numbers and general correctness of appearance, I elect to reduce the flanges as described in the next section. Occasionally, however, you come across the odd set of these wheels - the centres and axles of which are moulded integrally, don't forget - that have an appalling case of the staggers. My Jubilee was one such, with a tender that lolloped along like Long John Silver the morning after an all-night blinder on the contraband brandy.

A set of appropriate Kean-Maygib tender wheels was obtained as replacements. These come with 4mm scale standard 26mm long pinpoint axles, which will run happily enough in the plain bearing holes moulded into the Mainline tender sideframes. However, they are a very accurate fit, which means that you get neither vertical nor horizontal sideplay in any axle. I found that this led to derailments, so I used a 2mm drill to open out and slightly deepen the holes for the centre axle, introducing a little 'slop'. This gave the centre wheels about 1mm. total sideplay and around plus or minus half a millimetre vertical travel, which cured the problem.

Reducing Carrying Wheel Flanges

I've found that you can quite readily file down the flanges of the Mainline-type 'all in one' carrying wheels. As these wheels are integral with their axles, you obviously can't chuck them in a drill as suggested for removing tread blackening. The solution I use is far more Heath-Robinson even than this! To rotate these wheels so that I can attack them with a file, I use the bogie, carrying truck or whatever as a bearing block, and spin the wheels by pressing them against a rotating drum. This is nothing more prepossessing than an old cotton reel mounted on a quarter inch gutter bolt and chucked in a household electric drill. To give a 'grippy' surface to this improvised drive drum, I wrapped it in double sided carpet retaining tape (very useful stuff for the railway modeller, and only a couple of pounds for a big roll at your local carpet showroom).

The adhesive surface thus exposed is 'killed' a bit by handling it with grubby fingers, so that it's soft and slightly tacky.

With the drill clamped in my bench vice and running at its faster speed, the bogie complete with wheels is offered up to the spinning drum (watch your knuckles on the drill chuck). The wheelset to be filed down is pressed against the drum so that it spins, and a sharp flat needle file is applied to the edge of the flange to reduce its depth. As with the driving wheels, a nicely-

rounded finished profile is the aim. I do it all by eye, I'll confess, but if you have a vernier calliper gauge you can check to see how much you've reduced

The bogie wheels of Replica's B1 are acceptable in all respects but the overdeep flanges. So they were given the turning down treatment discribed in the text, for this pleasing result.

the flange by, and also to get all four flanges on the bogie to the same size. I aim for a finished flange depth of a bit over 0.5mm.

As always with these sorts of operations, *go gently;* never try and force the issue, and don't let any part of the job get at all hot. I lubricate the axle in the bogie with a drop of Vaseline - washed off afterwards - and I work on the tyres on both ends of an axle alternately, so that any heat from the friction of filing can dissipate. If you get a tyre too warm, it will come loose on the centre, and that's the kiss of death to *that* wheelset.

Keeper Plates

An aspect of most of split-frame spur-driven RTR chassis that I find particularly irksome is the fitment of a great deep keeper plate that obscures a lot of prototype daylight, and gives many models an oddly 'bottom heavy' look. Restoring the daylight and at least an approximation of a correct chassis outline is another upgrade that can make a lot of difference to the look of a model, but it's not always easy. The really aggravating thing is that, with few exceptions, these deep keeper plates serve no readily discernible purpose other than as a very clumsy mounting for the brake gear. In most cases, the bottom of the frames themselves is quite flat, although the final drive gear by the rear axle (and thus in in the firebox/ashpan area, where it could be hidden) often does protrude somewhat.

In my book, the loco worst afflicted by this problem is the Mainline/Replica GWR 2251, which really looks most odd. The keeper plate extends to within a few scale inches of the rail, which is completely at odds with the rather 'airy' nature of the prototype 2251 chassis. The problem is that on this engine, as on many others in the ex-Mainline range, the brake gear is moulded integrally with this keeper plate, which makes for a ticklish salvage operation and an awkward mounting problem. My pragmatic answer is as shown, where the moulded brakes and the chassis fore end detail are cut off the deep keeper plate, and fitted to a new, much less obtrusive plate made from 30thou. black Plastikard sheet.

The plastic from which these keeper

completely right! On other locos, where the error is not so pronounced, the reworked keeper plate can be considerably more effective.

Closing the Gap

We've already looked at the reduction of the loco - tender gap on conventionally powered models of the Mainline school of design, where there's no drawbar as such, only a rather large and obtrusive inverted hook. Tender

gether to give the required reduction in length. This brings the gap down to around 4mm .

Shortening Hornby's power-routing drawbar isn't quite so easy, but then it isn't half so necessary, as we're only looking to lose about a millimetre or so. To achieve this, remove the 8BA screw retaining the drawbar to the loco chassis, and extract the drawbar. This is made of quite thick and strong steel strip, and has a double edged phosphor-bronze wiper riveted to the ten-

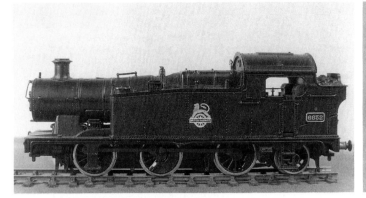

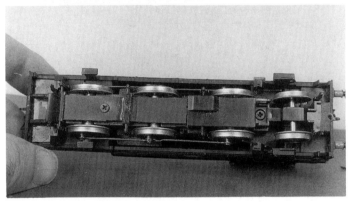
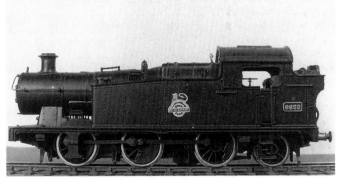

A fault shared by many small-wheeled locos from the old Mainline range is an over-deep keeper plate, which gives the engines a very 'bottom heavy' appearance, especially at the front end. My solution to this is to replace the forend of the keeper plate with some thin Plastikard; the rear part, covering the gears, has to stay. In some cases, such as the 56XX illustrated, there is also a front framing section moulded as part of this keeper plate, which becomes detatched when the plate is cut. I got around that snag by making the front framing part of the superstructure, gluing it in place with Cyano. The new centre section of the keeper plate is made from 20 thou. black plastikard, retained at the rear end by a tongue locating beneath the portion of the moulded plate covering the gears. The existing fixing screw was reused at the front end. To stop excessive wheel travel thick Plastikard blocks were cemented to the plate at the axle positions. Last job was to cut the brake gear from the discarded portion of the keeper plate; the segment of the old plate joining the two brakes was thinned by filing and cemented to the new plate.

plates are moulded is, unfortunately, one of the less responsive types so far as the solvent cements are concerned. This makes it difficult to get as good a bond as I would like between the brake hanger mouldings cut from the old Mainline moulded keeper, and the mounting on the new, finer effort. Mek is useless for this, and so far I have used Daywat Poly - with acceptable results. One just has to accept that the chassis detail is no longer quite as robust as it once was. A stronger solvent, such as 'Plastic Weld' (sold by Plastruct stockists) might do a better job.

This type of keeper assembly, with its relatively obtrusive vertical elements to provide brake hanger mountings, is still not a complete solution. In many cases, I fear, that only comes with the total replacement of the chassis by an etched job of scale outline. However, a standard chassis thus modified does look less wrong, even if it doesn't look

driven models, however, rely on some form of drawbar to propel the unpowered dummy loco. Hornby also use this drawbar to provide the earth return for the motor, via an insulated pin on the tender, wipers on the drawbar, and the un-insulated nearside wheels of the loco. Airfix do all their picking-up on the loco (wipers, thankfully, to all driving wheels) and connect the pickups to the tender motor with a fine twin core flex. To protect this against accidental breakage, they permanently couple loco and tender with a metal drawbar held with screws at both ends.

As this Airfix drawbar - which, in standard form, keeps the loco and tender more than 8mm apart - can very easily be reduced in length, it isn't quite the problem it might seem. Just undo the retaining screws at each end, remove the metal drawbar, cut it in two, and solder the two parts back to-

der end, which is delicate and must be preserved. As the coupling distance only needs reducing by about 1mm, it's not possible to drill a new hole, as was done on the Airfix drawbar. To change the centres in this case, I file the hole at the loco end of the drawbar oval, taking the metal out from the inner (tender) end. The resulting slop is taken up by filing the blackening off the drawbar, and soldering on a thin 8BA washer. The drawbar can then be refitted to the loco.

As before in concert with the closing up of the loco to tender gap, the fitting of a fall plate is a prime requirement. In addition to the fixed type already discribed it is possible to arrange fullplates to move as on the prototype. This is often a good idea on tender driven locos, and I illustrate a couple of ways of doing this in the sketch on the next page.

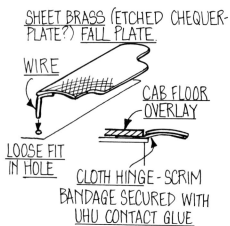

SHEET BRASS (ETCHED CHEQUER-PLATE?) FALL PLATE.

WIRE

CAB FLOOR OVERLAY

LOOSE FIT IN HOLE

CLOTH HINGE - SCRIM BANDAGE SECURED WITH UHU CONTACT GLUE

Moving Fallplate

Coupling Loops

I've already touched on the desirability of replacing the standard tension-lock couplings - with which all UK market RTR locos unfortunately come disfigured - with a simple wire loop, which maintains coupling compatibility but is a lot less noticeable. I would take the argument a stage further, and suggest again that it is possible to omit even these from the very-visible front end of many RTR express tender locos, without really impairing their operational potential significantly.

Among the many design faults of the British tension-lock as it has evolved, the ridiculous and highly unrealistic distance it puts between vehicles is one of the least tenable. In the same way that we are still apparently stuck with monstrous loco - tender gaps, a standard Bachmann or Replica wagon coupled to a tension-lock equipped RTR loco typically leaves a gap of 6mm between the buffers; that's 18 inches at full size, where the prototype allows, at most, a couple of inches.

By moving the position of the coupling loop on a modified loco, it is possible to close up the coupling distance as here. Unfortunately, you're still left with the unrealistic gap between other vehicles in the train

A gap half this wide will still get a train round almost any model railway curve while looking a whole heap better, and I set my loco coupling loops accordingly. I can see no reason why it should not be possible to design a version of the tension-lock which is both neater and less obtrusive, and which gives a far more realistic coupling distance. There is also a very strong case for evolving an industry-standard coupler mounting, to allow for interchangeable couplings without modification, as has been the case for years in the USA.

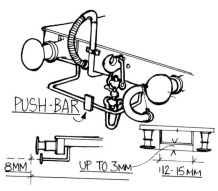

PUSH-BAR

8MM   UP TO 3MM   12-15 MM

Coupler Loops

Making Coupler Loops

As can be seen from the sketch and pictures, the basic coupler loop is a pretty simple affair, and a great deal less unsightly than the full house tension lock. The only real criterion for this loop is its height above the rails, and there's quite a bit of leeway even on that. I set mine at rail height plus 8mm, which equates to the level of the top of a normal tension-lock bar, but you can go the better part of a millimetre either side of this and things will still work OK. To make sure that the commercial type of couplings don't override (or underride) this thin wire in the pushing mode, I add a short vertical bar in the location that would be occupied by the loco's coupling hook, did it but have one.

I make the loop from either fine steel wire, as sold by Cove Models for point and signal control, or from 0.45mm or even 0.33mm brass wire, blackened with gun blue in all cases. The width of the loop isn't critical, so long as it's wide enough to accept the hook of an engaging tension-lock at any extreme. I usually opt for about 12mm, which is plenty. (Commercial coupler bars are about 16mm wide.) To bend these loops, I use a simple template.

Coupler loops can be a lot narrower then standard tension-locks, and hence a lot less obtrusive. They also allow the fitting of screw couplings, giving the best of both worlds.

Installing Coupler Loops

Mounting these loops is also a pretty simple matter, the preferred method depending rather on what you're mounting them to.

On replacement etched bogies or pony trucks, mounting is a simple soldering job, forming the loop to the required shape but arranging the fixing tails so that they can be soldered in place on top of the bogie or truck. Once they're firmly attached at the appropriate coupling distance, it's a simple enough matter to bend them up or down as necessary to get the right height above the rails.

Where the loops are being fitted to either a plastic bogie or truck, the tails of the loop are similarly formed, but given a 'melt-in' allowance so that they can be attached by this method, as described in Chapter 5 for grab rails and lamp irons.

On non-bogie locos and on tender

The coupler loops of the 57XX are simply melted-in to the remains of the original tension lock mounting block.

rears, the 'legs' of the loop are simply melted in to the cut-back remains of the tension-lock mounting block on the chassis in the same manner. In all cases, the aim is to get the distance of the loop out from the bufferbeam either level with, or slightly *behind* (for closer coupling) the plane of the buffer faces.

On diesels, I find that in most cases I can fit the loops to the bufferbeams on the body moulding rather than following the normal convention of bogie-mounted couplers. I can never see the need for this practice on anything other than trainset locos - all my US HO diesels have body-mounted couplers, and they will run on 18 inch radius curves if required. With a body-mounted loop, you can be sure that it's not going to get mixed up with all your beautiful bufferbeam detail, not at all the case when it's doing it's own thing in concert with the bogie.

Height adjustment of the loop is simply arranged by either melting the thing in a shade further, or by bending it up or down as appropriate to get the bar on or slightly below the 8mm datum. To a lesser extent, it is also possible to move the loop in and out in relation to the bufferbeam by tweaking the vertical legs too and fro.

Chassis Details

Nowadays, most RTR chassis come with a pretty complete set of chassis details. Brake gear, guard irons, sandboxes and so on are pretty much de riguer, and it is no longer necessary to worry about adding these elementary bits of locomotive anatomy to our models. Which is just as well, as trying to fit this sort of basic detail to the average cast block RTR chassis is the devil of a job.

This isn't to imply that all RTR chassis are completely detailed, nor that all the detail that is provided meets the mark. I quite often find that I need to add brake rigging to moulded-on brake hangers, for instance, while many models boast sandboxes but not necessarily the associated sandpipes. On other occasions, what should be filigree detail, such as sandpipes, injectors and other plumbing fittings, is either filled in solid, only partially represented, or moulded in a 'thick and chunky' format that's just not realistic.

So, I often find myself replacing moulded on sandpipes with wire, usually melted in to the moulded sandbox in my approved style. Pipework such as this, for obvious reasons, can't turn once it's in place, so I form a little kink in the melt-in tail so that the plastic has 'something to get hold of' in keeping the fixture firm. It's always important when installing sandpipes, even those located into plastic sandboxes, to make sure that they are well clear of wheel treads and rails, otherwise all sorts of electrical and mechanical mayhem can arise.

Injectors are the sort of detail below the footplate that can very often be fitted to the loco body and this, for instance, is what Dapol do with their J94 'Austerity' saddle tank. Many tender locos have this fitting tucked away behind the rear steps, and again, any representation can be made as part of the body. My usual method of representing a standard set of injectors is shown in the pipework sketch and the photo of the Jubilee. Again, this is a detail that many of the newer RTR locos are starting to include.

Other chassis pipework that may well need adding includes the cylinder drain cocks, already touched on, vacuum and steam heat lines and the loco - tender water and brake connections. These last are a delightful detail that is very easy to model, with wire hoses made like vacuum connections and glued or melted in to the loco or tender chassis as appropriate. The photo of the Jubilee illustrates the effect.

The last type of chassis detail that it's practicable to fit to RTR locos is the provision of special fittings such as AWS detector shoes or mechanical push-pull gear. AWS fitted locos will also need battery boxes, often mounted below the running plate; Replica include one on their B1, moulded inte-

The rear end of the Jubilee has acquired injectors - mostly hidden by the cab steps - and the loco/tender water hoses, just visible in the side view. These hoses are attatched to the tender as show in the second picture, and are bent to clear the loco chassis on curves.

grally with the offside cab steps. That's a pity, as not all B1s were AWS fitted, and not all that were had the battery box in that position. Such fittings are always best provided as 'add-ons', to be fitted by the user.

The GWR were the AWS pioneers, and many GW locos had very prominent detector shoes. There is a nice casting for this distinctive bit of kit, available from a number of different sources. It may need trimming for height before being glued in the appropriate location (reference photos!) with gel cyano or Araldite. Battery boxes can be bought cast, or simply made from Plastikard.

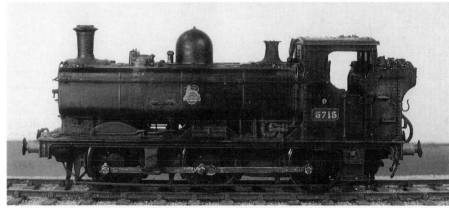

While the modified RTR chassis of the OO Replica Pannier 5762 can't quite match the kit built version of P4 sibbling 5715, the keeper plate modifications and improved detailing - especially the prominent AWS shoe - help make the difference less marked.

Tender Underframe Detailing

While we're about the loco chassis, it behoves us not to forget the underpinnings of the tender. Many of the same remarks apply, although I do find that a lot of RTR tenders do incorporate one annoying and rather too visible shortcoming. This is the moulding of the brake hangers just inside the tender frames, and hence way out of line with the wheel treads, especially on OO wheels. Even the Replica B1 offends on this count.

I find it worthwhile cutting these misplaced brake hangers away, and replacing them with correctly-positioned versions. For these, I either use etched brake hangers of the appropriate pattern, available separately from Perseverance and similar sources, or moulded plastic hangers from Gibson, Slaters or Cavendish. I fit the hangers on to wire pivots melted into the tender floor, as shown below, and finish the job off with wire cross rods and brass strip pull rods on the etched brakes, or the same thing in Microrod and Microstrip on the plastic ones.

Otherwise, I find that there's not a lot to do to tender underframes. Leaving aside the underpinnings of Hornby tender drives, which don't give you a lot of scope, I find most RTR tenders are very well furnished with waterscoops, air tanks and what have you. A lick of paint is usually all that I find I need to offer them; so:

A Lick of Paint

Indeed, at this stage of the proceedings, with the loco body carved-about, modified, added-to and redetailed, plus all the bits and pieces, adjustments and additions made to the chassis, the only thing needed now to complete the renaissance of our erstwhile RTR loco is a visit to the paintshop. And what a difference *that* can make...

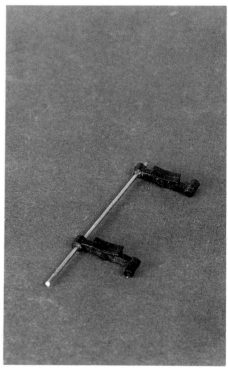

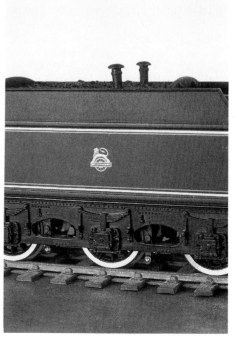

A common fault with RTR tender underframes is brake gear moulded integrally with the frames, and hence well out of line with the wheel treads. On the Jubilee's Fowler tender, I corrected this by carving away the offending items, and fitting new moulded plastic shoes from W&H Models. These were assembled as pairs on wire cross-hangers, which could then be soldered to fixed brake rigging made from square brass strip, melted in to the tender underframe moulding. The brakehangers were secured to their crossbars with Cyano. The resulting improvement is shown in the final picture.

Chapter Seven

Covering the Scars

Finish? What finish? On many occasions, the principle object of the exercise is to *get rid* of the 'bright and shiny' look that characterises so many RTR locos. It certainly didn't characterise the prototype finish of this humble shunter in BR days.

I don't know about you, but I find myself getting awfully blasé about the superb standard of finish we get on our RTR locos these days. It comes as a bit of a rude awakening when you have to try and match it for quality if your modifications to the model call for a bit of making good. However, as always, this apparent drawback can provide some opportunities as well as an undoubted challenge.

Of course, there are occasions when the model will need a complete repaint after modification. Apart from the obvious example of the R1 featured in these pages, where an unpainted body - obtained as a spare part and moulded, for some reason, in a fetching shade of coral pink - was used as the basis of the model, the need for a full paint job can be due to effects of major surgery, or in those cases where the 'starting point' model carried the wrong livery.

It matters not, as painting a model completely involves processes and techniques that are applied irrespective of the origins of the model. As the painting and lining of small scale models is covered in detail in Steve Barnfield's book on the subject, uniform, as they say, with this volume, there seems little point in my providing a skimpy account of the business here. What is of far more concern in the present context is the making good of factory paintwork, and the use of paint to improve and enhance the finished model.

Tools and Materials

Given that virtually all we're doing is to touch-in small areas of damaged paint, plus the odd bit of detail painting on existing or applied fittings, then our main tool is going to be the paintbrush, and a pretty small paintbrush at that. For this sort of work, as with almost any model painting, cheap squirrel hair brushes - as so often sold for this purpose - are worse than useless. On the other hand, there's no need to lash out the life savings on a set of best quality Kolinsky watercolour sables. The moderately priced synthetic bristle brushes provide just the 'middle path' that's needed.

I now make use of two basic ranges - the Daler-Rowney 'Dalon' series D77 nylon bristle watercolour brushes, and the same makers' slightly 'stiffer' series C10 'Cryla' range, intended specifically for use with acrylic paints. Handy, that, as I prefer acrylics for almost all model painting these days. For the sort of touch-in detailing work involved in an RTR conversion, we don't need a huge range of sizes. My usual selection starts with a D77 No.2, to cover the larger areas, and a No.0 'Cryla' for the twiddly bits. These two sizes are the minimum, although I also find the intermediate Cryla No.1 size useful, while for touching-in lining or lettering, a tiddly No.000 is useful; this is the only size for which I might lash out a few bob extra for a Rowney Series 40 sable.

As well as these pukka brushes, we also need a couple of less presentable specimens to undertake the rougher sort of job - dry brushing, as described in a page or two - plays merry hell with a good brush, so either keep a few older specimens that are past their prime for this particular form of abuse, or buy a small flat cheap bristle oil painting brush for the purpose; a student-quality No.1 Daler Rowney Series B36 'Bristlewhite' fits the bill quite nicely. The other low rent job is the application of weathering powders. I've got nothing against squirrels, but this is just about the only thing cheap squirrel hair brushes are good for. About a No.3 should do to apply the powder, with a biggish size - a No.6 or so - to brush it out. You can, once again, use a better brush that has been pensioned off, or something like the soft wide brushes sold for applying make-up.

You don't *need* an airbrush for the sort of paintwork involved in making good or improving RTR locos. However, if you do have access to one, it has its uses, not least among them the varnishing of the finished job. You can also use it, in conjunction with suitable masking, for spraying in any larger areas of paint that need to be altered or reinstated. However, neither role is exclusive to the airbrush; aerosol spray cans of varnish can be obtained from a number of different sources, while quite a few model paints are now also available in aerosol format if required. In fact, on all the models illustrated in this book, my sole use for the airbrush (I use a Badger 150) was to apply varnish, the least critical job, and one for which the aerosol is equally well-suited.

Paints and Varnishes

As with any other type of paintwork restoration, colour matching is the key to the making good of RTR paint finishes. Replica Railways are the only RTR maker to actually sell their 'house colours', as used on the models in their range. This should make touching-in a breeze, which it does, *provided* you can apply the paint in the right way. Unfortunately, these paints are really intended for spray finishing, and are rather too translucent for effective touching-in by brush, which is the usual restoration technique. The answer to this drawback is to underpaint the area to be touched-in with a suitable colour to 'fill out' the translucent top coat; a sort of pea green works in this way for the Replica GW green, and red oxide for the LMS crimson. I use Humbrol Hobby Acrylic matt paints for this purpose, shades 5036 and 5070 respectively.

These Humbrol Hobby Acrylic paints are now my firm preference for virtually all model painting work. They cover well, are available in gloss, matt, and now satin finishes, come in a very wide range of colours, are non-toxic and water based, and can be intermixed freely. I find that, in the vast majority of cases, I can mix the colours I need, a process I described in detail in the first volume of this series *Detailing and Improving RTR Wagons*. However, when working on RTR locos, I also find the original Humbrol enamel range very useful, especially the old Railway Colours - now, sadly, no longer available. Many of these were a surprisingly close match for a lot of the colours used on RTR models: Humbrol's GW loco green, for instance, is virtually identical to Bachmann's version of the same shade.

The shade we most often need when touching-in RTR locos is, however, black, a colour on which I'll have a bit to say in a paragraph or two. I find I use two basic black paints; in aerosol form, Humbrol's excellent 'Krylon', a fine satin spray black, and for brushwork and mixing - lots of mixing - the No.5033 matt black from the Hobby Acrylic range. Steer clear of the traditional car-type cellulose matt black sprays in this instance - these can easily craze plastic mouldings or any existing paint to which they are applied.

For detail painting and weathering, it's mostly the Hobby Acrylics again, with a typical selection used for RTR models including matt black 5033 and white 5034, silver 5011, red in both 5060 matt and 5019 gloss form, matt yellow 5024, matt blue 5025, matt light grey 5064, dark grey 5067, matt red oxide 5070 and matt earth 5029, the last two being essential weathering colours. The exceptions to my acrylic norm are metallics, for which enamels are better. I use Humbrol silver, gold and copper, plus the highly convincing burnishable 'polished steel'. The acrylic silver listed above I keep for mixing purposes.

Varnish is an essential and often overlooked part of the finishing process. It really does need to be sprayed on, as this not only gives a thin and uniform coat, but also permits a gradation in the degree of finish - anywhere from high gloss to dead matt. Varnish on a model - especially one that has had its paintwork touched-in or added to - has two important functions. Firstly, it protects the whole paint job, including transfer lettering or lining and extra fittings such as etched numberplates; secondly, and perhaps more importantly, it unifies the finish, bringing together the factory paint and brush applied remedial or additional work beneath a common surface texture. By tinting the varnish - only possible if you're using the airbrush, unfortunately - it can also serve used to 'tone down' the whole model as prescribed in the weathering section, getting away from the rather too punchy 'upfront' colours characteristic of many factory paint jobs.

There are umpteen types of varnish on the market that will do to protect and finish models, and I don't profess to have tried them all. Of those I have sampled to date, I find that the most useful are artists' ordinary fixative (which is a vinyl varnish, apparently), Humbrol matt enamel varnish, and the matt, satin and gloss varnishes from the Humbrol Hobby Acrylic range. Humbrol make a spray varnish in aerosol form, both matt and gloss; Railmatch also do aerosol varnishes in matt, satin and gloss. I'm not sure what types of varnish come in these sprays, but they seem effective on RTR finishes. Artists' fixative can also be obtained in aerosol format, but this is definitely different to the usual matt stuff that comes in bottles, drying much glossier. However, it's not a bad finish for a 'clean' loco.

Primers

Given that, for the most part, we're only dealing with plastic, and small areas at that, then we have no real need for primers for most of body touching-in work. However, when it comes to getting paint, particularly acrylic paint, to stick to metal, then a primer of some sort is a necessity. I use two approaches on metal parts, either chemically blackening them to give the paint a key (see below), or applying an etching primer in the same cause. The one I use these days is Replica Paints etching primer, but there are several alternatives. You can brush this primer on, but use a less than wonderful brush as it's not too kind to good ones.

Weathering Materials.

I weather my locos with a mixture of acrylic paint, chalk and the purpose-made Carr's weathering powders. I also make extensive use of chemical blackening agents for basic weathering of bright metal, as well as dulling down metal handrails, pipework, lamp irons and the like. You can buy a range of 'metal-dedicated' liquid blackening agents from Hubert Carr, or, like me, you can buy a pot of Phillips Gun Blue, an innocuous-looking turquoise paste which will blacken everything from a saint's name downwards. It is, however, highly toxic (as are the Carr's liquids), so needs handling with respect.

RTR Paintwork - Making Good

This is a process that starts during the modification work to the loco body, where care and attention paid to the matter of preserving and protecting the factory paint will be rewarded by the restricting of necessary finishing work to a bit of minor touching-in. It is surprising just what comparatively major operations can be carried out on a model without doing significant damage to the finish; it's also surprising just how effectively and unobtrusively the factory paintwork can be touched-in if you apply that finishing coat of varnish to give the common 'texture' to the painted surfaces. And, of course, a spot of toning down or weathering will help to blend together all elements of the model, including etched brass plates, jewelled lamps and the like.

Colour matching would appear to be the real nub of this business, but I have found that it's not as critical on locos (where we're usually only talking very small areas of paint to be touched-in) as it is on wagons where bigger areas like headstocks or underframes must match the existing body. In fact, more often than not you only have tiny patches to make good, as, for instance, along the top of a boiler where the mould part line has been scraped off. So long as the colour you use is close, the area applied is so small that it doesn't really 'register' with the eye to a sufficient extent to look wrong.

Where a bigger area, such as a cab side, is involved, then it is often better to repaint the whole thing, aiming to make the join along an edge, where the eye will anyway perceive a slight colour difference due to the different fall of light on the two surfaces. Similarly, if you do find that the top of a boiler or firebox has been ravaged to the extent that you need to repaint the whole area, try and arrange the join with the existing factory paint to fall along the line of the handrail or vacuum ejector pipe. It's surprising the degree of mismatch you can get away with when you disguise the meeting of the two shades of colour in this way.

I went into the business of colour matching techniques in considerable detail in the RTR Wagons book, and I'm not going to repeat every nuance here. The basic approach is to start with something that's somewhere near right, and tint it as required to get as close as possible to the correct shade. As a rule of thumb, it's better to start light and add black rather than trying to lighten a dark shade. Obviously, you'll only be able to mix paints of the same type, so if you're trying to adjust a Humbrol or Railmatch enamel, you will need some enamel tint shades as well.

Colour matching is, at best, a matter of refined trial and error. The best way is to paint test pieces for comparison with the factory colour you're trying to match. As most RTR loco bodies are moulded in black plastic, I use a piece of black Plastikard as my test piece. Paint your trial sample onto an edge of the Plastikard, let it dry (or blast it with a hairdryer, to speed things up), and compare it with the sample. Try to judge the match on three counts. Too light, or too dark? Too warm (reddish tinge) or too cold (blue tinge)? Too yellow, or not yellow enough? Back your judgement with a trial of the appropriate correction, using only a small quantity of your basic mix, so that you've still got plenty of original brew to play with if the first estimate turns out wrong.

I'm sorry that I can't be more definite about this, but it really is a process that comes down to a bit of practice and experiment, the keen use of a critical eye, and a bit of luck. The ultimate arbiter at the end of the day is whether or not the finished model looks OK to you. And that, to a large extent, comes down to your own perception and aspirations. Critics can either be invited to do better, or told to go boil their heads.

Applying Touch Up Paint

The object of this particular exercise is to try and get the texture of your paint as close to that of the original finish as possible, and also to avoid putting on too great a thickness or otherwise introducing raised or visible edges. Given that RTR models are spray painted, then trying to blend in new areas of paint applied by brush can be difficult - though a sprayed varnish finish does, as already noted, help to unify the differing surface textures.

Spraying

It is sometimes possible to spray in small areas of paintwork on an RTR model using an airbrush or aerosol, and if you are faced with a larger expanse of paint to apply, such as a tank or tender side, then it is probably the best approach, assuming you can come up with the right colour. If you have an airbrush, then the trial-and-error approach using painted - airbrushed, in this case - test patches will be perfectly effective. If you're relying on pre-mixed aerosols, however, you're obviously more limited. Although, that said, I find the Humbrol 'Krylon' spray matt black a good match for many all-black RTR locos.

If you only need to spray a small area, then the use of a spray mask can save a lot of work. This is simply a piece of paper with a suitably-sized hole cut in it, placed between the spray source and the model. The closer you place the mask to the model, the more abrupt will be the cut-off at the edge of your sprayed patch, not always desirable. If you hold the mask - the opening of which needs to be undersized in relation to the area you're spraying an inch or two off the surface, you can get a nice, soft, 'blended' edge to your patch. On the other hand, if you hold it actually in contact with the model, the result is a crisply cut off stencilled edge. A specially-formed contact mask is the device the RTR makers use to spray the different areas of livery colours on their models.

Brushwork

Where, as is usual, you can't touch in your models by spraying, but must use a brush, then it's desirable to get a surface which is close as possible to a sprayed finish - best done by flowing-on paint. Getting the paint to the right consistency for this is the main part part of the battle, and for this sort of work we need our paint surprisingly thick. Generally speaking, we also want good covering in one coat, and and for the paint to fill tiny scrapes and hollows in the factory finish.

The directions on most tins of paint - that injunction to 'mix the contents thoroughly' - are pretty dubious at the best of times. In this context, they're useless; what we want is a nice dip of good thick solid pigment from the bottom of an unmixed tin or pot, and only a drop or two of the carrier or varnish. Mix your paint in some suitable small container - I salvage those little pots that revolting UHT milk or cream comes in at most eateries these days. The little piece of black Plastikard also comes in handy to test the opacity of your touch-in paint; ideally, it should cover in one coat, but still be capable of being brushed-out thin at the edges. Getting the consistency right is half the battle, so it's worth fiddling about a bit in this cause.

I apply the paint with a suitable brush, the size of which is determined by the areas to be covered. A cabside or boiler top would call for the No.2 Dalon, but most typical touch-ins would be better accomplished with the No.0 Cryla. Panel painting uses a pretty ordinary brushing-out technique, but dealing with a toolmark or scratch is better accomplished with a 'spotting' technique, using the tip of the brush to apply little tiny blobs of colour, and letting them merge until the scratch or whatever is filled with paint. Let it be for a minute or two (not too long if you're using acrylics, which dry at 90 m.p.h. if you're not careful), then using a brush (wiped clean) gently and carefully brush out the edges of the repair to smooth it in with the rest of the paint.

In cases where new detail, let-in pieces or repair patches have been added to a moulded plastic body in white Plastikard or Microstrip, to get the new paint looking right you may well need to underpaint these white parts in a colour close to the shade of the main moulding, usually black on British RTR models. Where possible, I make Plastikard repairs or additions in black Plastikard, to save myself this particular trouble.

Enhancing Factory Paint

RTR locos are, undoubtedly, painted very well; but they're not always painted very *realistically*.This is, obviously, to keep costly handwork to a minimum, which is fair enough. It gives the modeller considerable scope not only to improve the look of his RTR model, but also to make it truly individual. There are also some 'toy train' traditions in the finishing of even the best of RTR models which can, to advantage, be done away with. Bright shiny wheel rims, shined-up fittings that never were, and things like unpainted handrails or turned brass safety valves will all benefit from a bit of attention from paintbrush or blackening agent.

The commonest shortcoming in the realism of factory paint is its lack of variety, particularly when it comes to black. Black is black is black, say the RTR makers. Black is usually anything but black, and varies a lot, say I. Take, for example, any all-black loco, such as the Replica B1 illustrated. As it comes, it's one overall, uniform, dense shade of black. Now look at a good photo - colour or black and white - of a *real* black loco. (I mean an in-service workaday steam engine, not some bulled-up and pampered preserved example). Hopefully, your picture will show the full range of subtle but significant variations in colour exhibited by a real engine, where the 'livery' colour - smokebox, footplating, cab roof,

chassis and wheels will all be slightly different shades of black.

Reproducing this subtle variety on a model has enormous benefits. It takes away the toylike look of a 'too perfect' finish, it adds significantly to the realism of the model, and it makes it unique, even among half a hundred examples from the factory pea pod. It is also sublimely easy to do. The process can be seen in the pictures of the LNER B1, where the various elements of the engine are simply brush painted in slightly different black mixes, using my favourite Humbrol acrylics. These are mixed to a normal flowing thin cream consistency, and applied with the No.1 and 2 brushes, brushing them out really thinly.

And the colours? Well, the smokebox is a very dead matt shade, black let down with grey 5067 and a touch of 5070 oxide and 5029 earth. This paint actually went on *after* the slightly satin varnish, to make sure it stayed dead matt. The footplating is in a warm black made with 5033 matt black and 5029 earth, about a 70 - 30 mixture. The cab roof is a greyer shade, a mix of black and 5067 dark sea grey, while the loco, bogie and tender frames are in a sort of oily black shade made much as for the footplate, but with more 5029 and a spot of 5070 oxide. The tender axleboxes, which are lined, have been spared this treatment.

Definitely not spared the treatment are the wheels, which are the part of any RTR loco most in need of paint. I

primed the bright, shiny rims with Replica etching primer, then brushed all the wheels with a slightly glossy black mix, made with 5033 matt, a drop of 5029 earth, and a generous dash of 5222 gloss varnish. Vive le différence! These subtle amendments to the factory finish transform the B1, as they will any similar plain Jane all-black engine, not to mention all the multi-coloured popinjay jobs. This subtle colour variegation makes RTR locos a good deal more realistic even before the weathering.

Detail Painting

This is the other area where RTR locos frequently fall down, for retail cost -v- handwork reasons. Most modern RTR locos, for instance, come with a full set of admirable cab fittings - but in unrelieved black throughout. Cut loose with the metallic paints, however, and you too can have a cab resplendent in a glory of polished metalwork - not to mention correctly painted interior and a wooden floor that looks like a wooden floor.

The same goes for all sorts of other little detail fittings about the locomotive's anatomy. Often, it will be a mat-

There's black and there's black; RTR black locos tend to come in a uniform shade that is both uninteresting and unrealistic. Varying the shade of black on different parts of the loco is a simple way of making it look convincing.

ter of picking things out in one of the various shades of black, but pipework, reversing reach rods and maker's plates may also call for metallics. On your crack express loco, a touch of Humbrol's burnishable 'polished steel' (toned down just a tad, I find) will give you a reach rod or buffer heads to be proud of. Most of my detail painting is undertaken with the acrylic paints and the No.1 Cryla brush, and is among the most satisfying aspects of the whole job. Again, this sort of work, carefully undertaken, can make a model not just pleasingly realistic, but also truly individual.

Toning Down and Weathering

Looking at a model from a normal viewing distance is equivalent to looking at the real thing through a couple of hundred yards of not entirely transparent atmosphere. Atmospheric dilution of colours is one way we have of telling how far away an object is, and diluting the colours of our models slightly, from 'full strength' foreground shades to slightly more receding 'middle distance' tones, will help their air of realism no end.

As already described in the notes on varnishing, I'll quite often achieve this toning down by tinting the varnish itself. If I can't do this, then I'll achieve a similar effect by brushing on a thin wash of acrylic colour across the whole model, with the occasional exception of any windows. This wash goes on before the varnish, and covers and polished metal fittings as well as the whole of the paint job.

The shade I use is a warm grey made by mixing equal parts of 5026 light grey, 5067 sea grey and 5029 earth. This is diluted until it's thin and watery, as thin as I can make it and still get it to stick to the model. It's brushed out thinly over the paintwork, wiping off any excessive build up with a tissue. A couple of light coats are much better than a single heavy application. It's worth experimenting on a scrap wagon body or similar to get the hang

Any loco will look better if its 'up front' factory finish in toned down with a wash of dilute acrylic, or sprayed with a coat of tinted varnish. 'Amethyst' represents a clean loco, but even so both finish and colouring are subdued in the cause of realism.

of this wash - it really is only the very faintest tinting and dulling of the underlying colours that we're after.

Weathering

The toning down process is the foundation of any weathering job, and is probably the most important and effective part of the whole business. Only when this has been satisfactorily achieved do I come on to consider what most people mean when they talk of weathering - the simulation of dirt, pollution, wear and tear and corrosion about the anatomy of a locomotive. While this process is a vital step in the quest for realism, it's all to easy to overdo it, and end up with a loco that looks as though it's just been dragged out of a scrapyard.

Good reference pictures, colour if possible, are a great help in executing a really convincing weathering job. I often elect to make my models as 'portraits' of a specific prototype engine, and that will extend to the weathering. Keen observation and a basic working knowledge of where locos leak,

get knocked, have things spilt on them and accumulate dirt will also help when it comes to making your model look like a real engine, warts and all. On the same general point, I find it's important to weather a loco as a whole, rather than treating the chassis and superstructure differently, at different times. Keep the model in one piece as far as possible during the weathering processes.

Weathering Techniques

Just as the weathered appearance of a real loco is the result of a lot of factors and influences acting on the original finish, so a number of methods are needed to replicate the accumulated effect. As with the toning washes, it's best to build up weathering gradually, rather than trying to slap it all on in one go. There are four basic weathering techniques that I use - normal painting, washes, dry brushing and powders. They are usually used in succession in that order, starting with the picking out of parts of the loco in 'weathered' colours rather than livery

The 56XX, in its raw state on the left, received the full treatment : Variegated shades of black, detail painting, a toning wash and drybrush and powder weathering.

shades.

I suppose that my variegated blacks are a start of this process, but I find that there are quite a few other parts of the loco that need to be painted in a shade that has more to do with a weathering influence than any colour that might have been applied intentionally. Rust on brake blocks, ashpan sides and other areas where paint might not be expected to stay put is one example, as is the oily silver/brown/grey shade of acrylic that I use for many parts of the motion, especially when painting in moulded plastic slidebars and toning down valve gear generally. For painting black plastic slidebars, I use the mixture - roughly one third each of matt black 5033, matt earth 5029 and silver 5011 - at full strength. For bright metal rodwork or plated cast crossheads, I thin it a bit, and flow a translucent coat over the metal valve gear parts. Shiny valve gear exists only in fairyland or on preserved railways.

Basic accumulations of dirt or an all-over coat of grime call for more dilute washes of acrylic, in a brownish shade compounded mostly of 5029 earth and 5067 dark sea grey. Again, the paint is put on very thinly, building up the

Carr's 'rust' weathering powder is pretty potent stuff and can be rather dominant. If you get too much on, as I have with the Pug here, the joy of is that you can simply brush the excess off again.

eking out retirement in this punishing role. If you do use your very best new brush for a lot of dry brushing, it will

Drybrushing acrylic paint upwards over the lower part of the Jubilee's running gear, footplate and boiler simulates track dirt thrown up. The rather stark effect in the photograph is toned down and unified by a final overall wash of dilute acrylic, followed by a mist of tinted varnish.

effect with several very light coats. I often wipe most of the paint off again with a tissue, which gradually leaves a build-up of colour in those less accessible places where such grime tends to collect. Often, I'll introduce the paint at these points, then brush it outwards from there.

Drybrush Weathering

More specific and concentrated accumulations of dirt are the province of dry brushing, a very basic weathering technique. Matt acrylic paints are the usual medium, but used fairly thick and 'dry' on this occasion. You also need a suitable brush for this technique, as prescribed in the shopping list at the start of this chapter. I generally use a once-good Dalon No.3, now

soon become a once-good specimen!

The technique is very simple - you pick up a very small quantity of paint on the brush, get rid of most of that by brushing out on a tissue, and only when the brush is barely moist with the remainder of the paint do you let it near the model. Drybrushing relies on the surface textures of the model to drag tiny parcels of paint off the brush, and so is used either to 'shade' the model - by brushing darker tones up from below, or to 'highlight' by using a pale tint from above, If you haven't tried it before, I recommend experimenting on a wagon body before cutting loose on your best sixty quid loco. Again, the aim is to build up the effect gradually in as controlled a manner as possible, so take it steady and keep a critical eye on the results. The pictures

should give an idea of the possibilities.

Powder Weathering

The use of powders - specifically, ground artists' pastel chalks, or pure weathering pigments - is a useful and subtle technique, particularly for adding or accentuating textures. It is excellent for simulating the build up of 'road dirt' - the mud and dust flung up from the trackbed as the loco passes over it. The exact shade, will, if we're being pedantic about it, depend on the prevailing ballast and soil colours in the district in which the loco is supposedly running; in practice, a grey/brown hue with a touch of rust-red looks about right. If you're using Carr's weathering powders, watch the reds generally and the red ochre 'rust' in particular; it's a very strong and dominant colour, and can very easily swamp the other shades.

I prefer to mix my weathering powders to get the shade I'm after rather than taking the descriptions on the packets at face value. I put them on with a small, soft paintbrush, working with small quantities of powder. I then brush it out with a much larger brush - the No.6 squirrel hair or an old make-up blusher brush pinched from that table-thing with the mirror on it in the bedroom. Again, the approach is to build up the effect gradually, using successive slight applications of colour rather than going mad in one go. Go mad slowly, like me! If you do get too much on, you can wash it all off with clean water and a tiny drop of washing up liquid (to lower surface tension), and start again.

I find that these weathering pigments stay put pretty well of their own accord, but if you're worried that they might go AWOL, then a very light spray of artists' fixative will seal them in

Classic 1950s war-stripes on the Boston & Maine F7A, weathered with toning wash, drybrush and powder to represent a hard working 'in service' freight loco.

place. The matt fixative in a bottle is best for this, applied with an airbrush if at all possible. If you don't have such an animal, art shops also sell simple mouth-blown spray tubes for applying this fixative; they're surprisingly effective. The aerosol stuff does work, but the spray is a bit on the vigorous side, especially in a new tin. And, as noted, it tends a bit toward glossiness on a non-absorbent surface such as paint; it's really intended for use on paper.

Watermarks and Limescale

These are two weathering features that can, if properly applied, look stunning. They are, however, awfully easy to overdo. The common watermark is the washdown resulting from spillage when tender or sidetanks are filled to overflowing, and this will often 'cut across' other weathering. Replicating such an effect can be achieved - by wiping or by washing off the overall 'toning down and dirt addition' application of thinned acrylic paint from the affected areas. This must be done at the time the wash is being brushed on, as once acrylic paint is dry, it's waterproof. It can, however, be removed by *gently* burnishing with a propelling pencil type fibreglass brush, so this is an alternative technique.

The actual watermark can then be brushed on, using a wash of very pale grey which is allowed to run naturally

Water spillage and the ensueing lime stains are represented by a mixture of drybrushing and toning wash. It's easy to overdo these affects which really need to be very subtle, as on the 14XX.

down the side of the tank or tender side. Make sure the model is standing on a level surface when you do this - watermarks that defy gravity look most odd! I reinforce the watery look by brushing on a little matt fixative and letting it run down in the same way. This is a tricky effect to bring off, so try it out on a scrap vehicle or piece of Plastikard first.

Limestreaking is simply achieved with matt white acrylic paint used wet, but very, very sparingly. Very limey water was virtually never used for locomotive purposes after the advent of the softening plant, so don't overdo the fallout. A faint suggestion of lime-white

around the injector overflows, safety valves, leaking joints and the washout plugs are all that is needed.

Painting Wheels and Valve Gear.

Wheels are fiddly things to paint and can be time consuming. It's also a job to get paint and weathering materials to stick to the shiny plated rims of RTR wheels. I overcome this drawback by brushing on Replica's etching primer before painting the wheel-rims, as in the picture on the next page. You can speed up the painting of wheel-rims considerably by applying the paint to the revolving wheels, clamping the chassis in the vice and applying power via some test leads.

Don't forget that the backs of the wheels also need priming and painting if possible, which it is in the case of the Jubilee and all other locos using the Mainline style of split-frame pick up. Once again, the painting of wheel-backs can be quickly accomplished with the chassis under power. Wheels need weathering, too, so the same processes of toning down, drybrushing and powdering are applied. I do this at the same time as I weather the valve gear and the rest of the chassis.

Chassis Painting.

The finish of the cast RTR chassis block will also benefit from a coat of paint, followed by the picking out of detail and the usual toning-down and weathering. Ashpans, particularly, should have a nice rusty finish, while water and oil spillage and road dirt can be represented withg paint and powders. Valve gear can be washed over with a grey-brown oily shade of acrylic, and dry-brushed with road dirt, as in the picture.

Finishing Touches.

These are the little, final details added at the time the loco is nearing the end of the paint job, which can bring the whole thing to life. The importance of lamps I've already touched on; Springside and Kenline do excellent jewelled cast lamps that, weathered down a bit, look very convincing. They can be made removable by drilling a clearance hole for the lamp iron into the bottom of the lamp, and sitting them *on* the iron rather than in front of or beside it.

Fire irons are simply made from wire and shim, as in the sketch. Other little touches include oil cans, tea billies and snap bags hanging in the cab, and the coal-watering hose dangling out of the cab doorway or hung over the sidesheet. Weather sheets can be simulated with tissue paper stained an appropriate grey-brown with acrylic paints, then 'tied up' with five amp fuse wire and cyano'd in place.

Adding these little details can really set an RTR model apart. And is the Patient Feeling Better?

Setting an RTR model locomotive apart, giving it individuality and character, and making it more satisfying to own, operate and look at, is the ultimate aim of my whole approach to working with modern mass-produced models. I get a lot of satisfaction out of it, and at the end of the day I find that I have been able to assemble a pretty presentable loco stud without spending too much in time or money, neither of which commodity is in generous supply hereabouts. I hope that these techniques will enable you to reach the same happy goal.

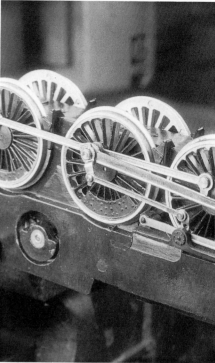

Painting wheels is quicker under power.

Painted and weathered chassis.

68

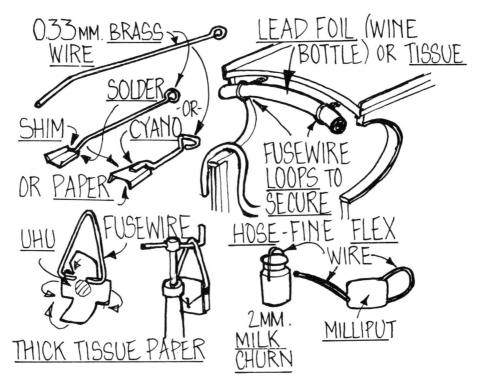

0.33MM. BRASS WIRE

LEAD FOIL (WINE BOTTLE) OR TISSUE

SOLDER

-OR-

SHIM

CYANO

OR PAPER

FUSEWIRE LOOPS TO SECURE

UHU   FUSEWIRE

HOSE-FINE   FLEX WIRE

THICK TISSUE PAPER

2MM. MILK CHURN

MILLIPUT

Detail

Headcode lamps are an important front end detail on any loco, but need weathering to blend in with the rest of the model. These are Spring side jeweled lamps.

Details add character.

List of Suppliers

Leaving aside the odd foreigner, the models worked upon and described in this book came from one or other of the main UK makers or importers.

In the case of those suppliers retailing models made in the far east, there is some overlap, especially with respect to the remains of the old Palitoy 'Mainline' and 'Airfix' ranges. Some models are thus available under more than one brand-name, although not always to the same specification. Sorry if this is confusing, but it's definitely not my fault!

Bachmann Industries (Europe) Ltd., Moat Way, Barwell, Leicestershire, LE9 8EY.
Wide listing developed from the old Mainline range, but now with a lot of new models. The only manufacturer currently engaged on large-scale serious development work on new locomotives. Widely available - sold by virtually all model shops. More recent productions are made in mainland China (Peoples Republic of), with slight loss in quality of finish, but bonus of low prices. Latest generation of chassis are mostly excellent runners.

Dapol Model Railways Ltd. Well Street, Winsford, Cheshire. CW17 1HW.
Tel: 0606 592122.
Most of the old Airfix range, plus a few bits of Mainline and several introductions on their own account, including GW Hawksworth 'County' 4-6-0, LBSC Terrier, J94 Austerity and the 'Pug'. Now also have the old Wrenn range, plus bits of British Trix. Availability a bit patchy, not all shops stock. Dapol have their own retail department, and can usually help. Dapol will also happily supply almost any part as a spare - watch their adverts in the model railway press.

Hornby Hobbies Ltd., Westwood, Margate, Kent, CT9 4JX.
The grandaddy of these ranges, celebrating its 44th. birthday in 1994.
Took over the even older Hornby-Dublo range in 1965, but these were hived off as Wrenn, now part of Dapol. Hornby have not moved toward the adult scale model field to the same extent as Dapol, Replica and Bachmann, so their models incorporate more compromises. Available just about everywhere, and mostly Made in Britain.

Lima Model Railways. Imported by Riko International Ltd., 13-15a, High Street, Hemel Hempstead, Hertfordshire, HP1 3AD.
Made in Italy and, like Hornbby, not quite so far down the 'scale' road as the others. Share with Hornby a tendency to make everything too high off the rail, with very coarse wheels. Very good body mouldings and finish, though. The strength of their range is in the diesel locos. Very widely available.

Replica Railways. Station Yard, Lambourn, Berkshire, RG16 7PH.
The smallest of the suppliers, Relica state on their literature that they 'manufacture detailed scale models for adult collectors'. As with Bachmann, Replica's roots lie in the old Mainline range; there is considerable overlap between their listing and Bachmanns, although Relica do have some newer models which are exclusive to them, most notably the GWR 'Modified Hall'. Replica also seem to opt for a higher specification of finish, but, so far, lack the flywheel drive. Widely available through shops. Bodies available separately as spares.

Parts Suppliers

Not a complete listing, inevitably; these are the ones I know about and use. Probably just as many I've missed out. Sorry!

Alan Gibson (Workshop), The Bungalow, Church Road, Lingwood, NORWICH, Norfolk, NR13 4TR. Tel: 0603 715862. (8 a.m. - 6 p.m. Mon - Sat).
Wheels, brass and whitemetal detail castings, turned brass handrail knobs, sprung buffers, etched parts, moulded plastic brake gear, and goodness knows what else. Catalogue a must. Available from most model shops or direct by mail order (credit cards taken). Attends major shows.

Branchlines, P.O. Box 31, Exeter, EX4 6NY. Tel/Fax 0392 437755. Credit cards taken.
Detail parts, including screw couplings, also chassis kits for some RTR locos. 145% solder, flux.

London Road Models. 1, The Avenue, North Street, Romford, Essex, RM1 4DL. 0708 761592
Detail parts, including cab fittings, plus 145° solder and flux.

Ferdale Forge, Burghfield Common, Reading, Berks. Tel: 0734 832402
Handrail knobs - available through many shops.

Comet Models, 105, Mossfield Road, Kings Heath, BIRMINGHAM, B14 7JE.
Tel: 021 443 4000 or 021 449 5038 (24hr. Ansaphone).
Etched bogies, pony trucks, cast/etched cylinders, very good motoion sets and valve gears, complete locomotive chassis kits for most RTR loco bodies, tender undeframe kits. Available through model shops or direct by mail order (Credit Cards taken). Attend many shows.

Crownline Models Ltd., 8, Rame Terrace, RAME CROSS, Cornwall, TR10 9DZ. Tel/Fax. 0209 860157 (10 a.m. - 6 p.m. Mon - Fri.).
A huge range of conversion kits and parts for RTR locos, especially Hornby. Many etched and cast detailing parts. Catalogue a must.
Some shops, mail order, attend larger shows.

Jackson-Evans. 4, Dartmouth Road, Wyken, COVENTRY, CV2 3DQ.
Tel: 0203 443010.
The name and numberplate people - list runs to several thousand different types, 'Big-4' pre-nationalisation, BR, including post-TOPS contemporary, plus narrow-gauge, industrial & freelance. Also shed and builders plates. Pre-cut, pre-coloured, excellent and inexpensive.

Also range of cast, etched and turned fittings including balance weights and smoke deflectors. Most shops can supply, or direct mail order. Some shows.

A1 Fittings. Howes of Oxford, 9 - 10, Broad Street, OXFORD, OX1 3AJ.
Tel: 0865 242407 Fax: 0865 242807.
Specialising in detailing parts for contemporary prototype. Also A1 Railmatch paints, likewise biased for modern scene. Available through good mosel shops or direct by mail order (Credit cards taken). Some shows also.

Craftsman Models, 1, St. Johns, WARWICK, CV34 4NE. Tel: 0926 402932.
Conversion and detailing parts - many etched - for steam, diesel and electric locos. Good for breathing more life into Hornby diesels, as well as providing the finest etched windscreen wipers. Available through model shops or direct by mail order.

American Bits & Pieces, Detail Associates, Details West, Cal-Scale, Precision Scale and Tichy Train Group, all from Victor's, 166, Pentonville Road, LONDON N1 9JL. Tel: 071 278 1015. Fax: 071 278 8783.

Tools & Materials Suppliers.

Again, not a complete list - these are the ones I use and can recommend.

ACME Model Co. P.O. Box 69, Hampton, Middx, TW12 3NA Tel: 081 979 0672. (No credit cards)
The XURON snips, also all North West Short Line tools from U.S.A.
145° solders and fluxes available from London Road Models or Branchlines.

John K Flack, 1, Meadow Bank, Kilmington, AXMINSTER, Devon, EX13 7RL.
Tel: 0297 32398.
Evergreen Styrene - sheet, strip (huge range of sizes) and rod. Plus milled brass strip and wire of all sorts, small screws, some tools. Mail order only, excellent service. Catalogue a must.

Eileen's Emporium. 55, Reedsdale Gardens, Gildersome, LEEDS, Yorkshire. LS27 7JD. Tel: 0532 537347.
As for John K, but not so much styrene and a lot more tools. List a must. Mail order, attends a lot of shows in the north of the country.

Shestos. Nathan Shestophal Ltd., Unit 2, Shapcote Trading Centre, 374, High Road, Willesden, LONDON NW10 2DH. Tel: 081 451 6188.
The tool people. Almost everything in my tool lists can be obtained here.

Dolphin Crafts. 1, Mill Street, CHAGFORD, Devon, TQ13 8AW. Tel: 0647 432257.
Paint, including Humbrol Krylon spray and all the Hobby Acrylics range, brushes of all the types listed, varnishes, spray fixatives.